Welcome

120   160

62   148

DECIDING WHICH RECIPES TO USE FOR OUR FIFTH – yes, you heard me, fifth! – annual yearbook is both brilliant and difficult at the same time. Over the last 12 months we've built up such a spectrum of tasty recipes, spanning all seasons and occasions which was incredible to look back through, but made it nigh on impossible to decide what to include! After much deliberation, we've pulled together this beautiful selection of dishes and I hope you love them all as much as we do – we've gone for things you'll want to cook again and again; treats for special occasions and simple staples to help you out in the week. From soups and starters, to meaty marvels, fantastic salads and veggie dishes that'll blow you away, there's something for everyone. The year ahead is looking busier than ever already, and I can't wait to get started… watch this space! Big love,

Welcome to our fifth *Jamie* magazine yearbook, which offers a great way to cook your way around some of our favourite recipes from the 2013 issues. As ever, we've divided them up into chapters and added some extra tips and recipe ideas to give you added inspiration in the kitchen. Above, you'll see some of my favourite recipes to come out of our test kitchens – a chocolate chai sandwich cake just made for afternoon tea; butterflied leg of lamb with a Mexican-style marinade, perfect for a summery barbecue; fruity Tiki Miki cocktails; and a great Spanish-style aubergine, pepper and jamon salad. As always, our thanks go to Jamie and everyone else who helps create the recipes, and to the photographers who bring them to life on our pages. Enjoy your cooking, eating and drinking, wherever you are!

Follow Jamie on Instagram and YouTube!

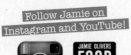

Editor at Large

Editor

3

26

152

159

58

107

117

92

132

45

Contents

Fresh & Healthy

Our mission at Gousto is to make it easy to cook quick and healthy meals at home with fresh ingredients. Each week, you choose recipes online and we deliver everything you need in pre-measured portions.

how to redeem your £15 coupon

1. visit us at **www.gousto.co.uk**
2. select your box
3. enter your code **RECIPES15** at checkout to save £15
4. select your recipes

£15
-- off --

✓ **FREE** delivery

✓ **healthy meals**

BREAKFASTS, SNACKS & STARTERS

It's not all about the main course. Whether you're looking to kick-start your day, grab something to keep you going or wow your dinner guests with an impressive entrée, we've got your light bites covered

Gousto

Simply cook

GOODNESS BREAKFAST WITH MAPLE PEARS

Head starts

There's no denying that a bowl of grains or oats makes a good start to the day. All that low-GI goodness really fills you up, releasing its energy throughout the morning to keep you satisfied until lunch. To add a tasty new dimension to your grains, seeds and nuts, toasting is in order: prepare a jar of your favourite mix in advance by simply spreading it out on a baking tray and giving it a blast in a hot oven for 15–20 minutes. Then, when you're running for your train in the morning, all you need to do is add fruit (fresh, dried or poached) and milk (either heat it and treat your mixture like porridge or splash it over ice cold). Nuts and grains pair beautifully with warm spices such as cinnamon, allspice, cardamom and nutmeg, so don't be afraid to experiment. For a brilliant breakfast that you can pack up into a flask and take with you, use your favourite grains whizzed up into a creamy smoothie with fresh fruit and yoghurt.

GOODNESS BREAKFAST WITH MAPLE PEARS

Serves 4-6
- 100g each of oats, millet flakes, barley flakes and quinoa
- 40g pumpkin seeds
- 40g sesame seeds
- 2 tbsp honey
- 800ml-1 litre almond milk
- Flaked almonds, to serve

Maple pears
- 2 pears, cored and sliced
- 1 tbsp maple syrup, plus extra

1 Preheat the oven to 180C/gas 4. Mix the oats, flakes, quinoa and seeds in a bowl, then scatter over a roasting tray. Toast in the oven for 20 minutes, checking and shaking every 5 minutes to ensure it browns evenly. Cool and store in a jar until breakfast.
2 Put the toasted mixture in a pan, along with 800ml of almond milk and simmer for about 10 minutes, or until the grains are tender. Add the extra 200ml of almond milk to loosen slightly, if you like.
3 Meanwhile, heat the pears and maple syrup in another pan over a medium heat for 5 minutes, until warmed through. Serve your toasted grains topped with a warm slice of pear, a drizzle of maple syrup and flaked almonds.
Per serving 589 cals, 17.5g fat (2.5g saturated), 19g protein, 81.6g carbs, 23.6g sugars

ROASTED GRAPES WITH CHEESE

Serves 8
- 1kg black grapes, on the vine
- 1 tbsp golden caster sugar
- A few sprigs of thyme, leaves picked
- Extra virgin olive oil
- A splash of red wine vinegar
- 75g crème fraîche
- 50g Westcombe cheddar, roughly chopped into large chunks
- 250g Tunworth (or any good camembert-style cheese)
- 1 bunch of sage, leaves picked
- Fresh bread and walnuts, to serve

1 Preheat your oven to 220C/gas 7. Place the grapes in a large roasting tray, sprinkle with the sugar and thyme and drizzle with olive oil and vinegar.
2 Roast the grapes for 5-10 minutes, keeping an eye on them and turning when necessary, until they are just starting to catch and burst open.
3 Remove the tray from the oven and spoon dollops of crème fraîche over the grapes, scatter over the cheddar chunks, then tear up the Tunworth and nestle the pieces among the grapes.
4 Drizzle the sage leaves with olive oil and scatter over the top. Return the dish to the oven for 5 minutes, or until the cheese starts to melt.
5 Serve in the middle of the table with a loaf of your favourite bread, a bowl of walnuts, and a lovely bottle of red.
Per serving 240 cals, 14g fat (9g saturated), 7g protein, 22g carbs, 21g sugars

ROASTED GRAPES WITH CHEESE

PORK, SAGE & CHESTNUT ROLLS

PEPPER & CHORIZO TORTILLA

VENISON, MUSHROOM & JUNIPER ROLLS

PORK, SAGE & CHESTNUT ROLLS

The perfect marriage of flaky pastry and stuffing ingredients makes this a great treat for Christmas – but they will taste amazing any time!

Makes 20 mini rolls

- 1 onion
- 50g roasted and peeled (or vacuum-packed) chestnuts
- 14 sage leaves, plus 20 to decorate
- 450g minced pork
- 1 tsp mustard seeds
- 500g puff pastry
- 1 egg, beaten

1 Preheat the oven to 200C/gas 6. Dice the onion and roughly chop the chestnuts and sage. Mix well in a bowl with the minced pork and mustard seeds.
2 Roll out the puff pastry to 60 x 18cm, then cut into 2 long strips. Lay half the mince mixture down the centre of each strip. Brush the long edges with the beaten egg, then fold them over and press together to seal. Cut each log into 5cm pieces and place on baking sheets lined with baking paper.
3 Brush the tops with beaten egg, add a sage leaf to each piece, brush with egg again and bake for 35 minutes, until golden, puffed up and cooked through.

Per sausage roll 151 cals, 8.3 fat (3.9g saturated), 6.4g protein, 10.6g carbs, 0.9g sugars

PEPPER & CHORIZO TORTILLA

Serves 6-8

- 4 tbsp olive oil
- 2 baking potatoes, about 400g in total, very finely sliced
- 1 onion, finely sliced
- 1 red pepper, finely sliced
- 150g chorizo, cut into chunks
- 6 eggs
- 2 tbsp chopped parsley

1 Preheat the oven to 180C/gas 4. Heat 2 tablespoons of the olive oil in a large ovenproof frying pan (a 30cm-diameter pan is ideal) and gently cook the potatoes, onion and pepper for 10-15 minutes, until softened and the potato is almost cooked through.
2 Add the chorizo and cook for a further 5 minutes. Beat the eggs in a large bowl, stir in the parsley, then add the potato and chorizo mixture. Let the mixture sit for a minute or two while you heat the remaining oil in the frying pan.
3 Once the oil is hot return the mixture to the pan and cook for 5-7 minutes until it is set around the edge, then transfer to the preheated oven for another 5-7 minutes to finish cooking. Invert onto a large board or plate, allow to cool, then cut into wedges and serve.

Per serving 303 cals, 21g fat (5.3g saturated), 13.7g protein, 16.5g carbs, 4.5g sugars

VENISON, MUSHROOM & JUNIPER ROLLS

If you can't get venison, pork mince will also work – or use a mixture of both for double the delicousness.

Makes 8 large rolls

- Olive oil
- 1 onion, diced
- 1 large garlic clove, chopped
- 1 tsp crushed juniper berries
- 125g chopped mushrooms
- 450g venison mince
- 500g puff pastry
- 1 egg, beaten

1 Preheat the oven to 200C/gas 6. Heat a drizzle of olive oil in a pan and fry the onion until soft. Add the garlic, juniper berries and mushrooms, then fry for 5 minutes. Remove from the heat, season and leave to cool. Once cool, mix with the venison mince and season well.
2 Roll out the puff pastry to 48 x 22cm, then cut into 8 rectangles. Lay the mince mixture down the centre of each, brush the long edges with beaten egg, then fold over lengthways and press to seal.
3 Place on a baking sheet lined with baking paper, slash the tops three times diagonally, brush with beaten egg and bake for 35 minutes, until golden and the filling is cooked.

Per sausage roll 333 cals, 18.1g fat (8.4g saturated), 17.9g protein, 23.8g carbs, 1.9g sugars

ONION BHAJIS

Pastry
- 500g flour, plus extra for dusting
- 250g butter, chilled and diced
- 1 beaten egg

Béchamel sauce
- 600ml milk
- 2 bay leaves
- 60g butter, melted
- 4 tbsp flour
- 150g cheddar, grated
- ½ tsp grated nutmeg

1 To make the pastry, place the flour and butter in a food processor with a pinch of salt and blend until it's the texture of fine breadcrumbs. Pour in the beaten egg, then gradually add 3-5 tablespoons of water to make a smooth dough. Shape into a disc and put in the fridge for 30 minutes.
2 Now for the filling. Heat the butter and oil in a large frying pan over a medium heat, add the leek and cook until softened, about 5 minutes. Add the potatoes and peas and cook for 5 more minutes. Transfer the mixture to a bowl, add the ham, season well and stir together well. Set aside.
3 To make the sauce, heat the milk and bay leaves in a pan over a low heat. In another pan, melt the butter over a low heat, then whisk in the flour until combined. Slowly ladle the hot milk into the flour mixture (discarding the bay) and whisk continuously until thickened. Remove the sauce from the heat and leave to cool slightly, then stir in the cheese and nutmeg. Add to the vegetable and ham filling and mix well.
4 Preheat the oven to 200C/gas 6. On a floured surface, roll out the pastry to 3mm thick. Using a 10cm pastry cutter, cut out 12 circles. Spoon a little filling into the centre of each and brush the edges with the beaten egg. Bring the pastry edges up around the filling, crimp with your fingers to seal, then brush all over with more beaten egg.
5 Place the pasties on a baking tray and bake for 10 minutes in the preheated oven, then turn down the oven to 180C/gas 4 and cook for a further 5-10 minutes, or until golden brown.
Per serving 252 cals, 14.7g fat (8.8g saturated), 7.8g protein, 21.2g carbs, 1.9g sugars

ONION BHAJIS
So easy to make, so delicious to eat, so much better than going for takeout!
Serves 4 as a side
- 200g gram flour
- 1 tsp turmeric
- 1 tbsp coriander seeds, crushed
- 5 cardamom pods, seeds removed and crushed
- 1 tsp garam masala
- 1 red chilli, deseeded and finely chopped
- 2 large onions, sliced into wedges
- Vegetable oil

1 Prepare the batter by mixing the flour, spices and chilli in a bowl with a pinch of salt and pepper. Add cold water, a little at a time, until you have a thick batter. Stir in the onions, making sure they're well coated. Meanwhile, half fill a medium-sized heavy-based pan with oil and set it over a medium heat. Test the oil is hot enough by adding a drop of batter – if it fizzes straight away, it's ready. In batches, gently drop spoonfuls of the bhaji mix into the pan. Use a slotted spoon to turn them, then, when they're golden all over, transfer to kitchen paper to drain. Serve straight away as a snack, or with your favourite curry.
Per serving 313 cals, 16.7g fat (1.8g saturated), 11.4g protein, 32.4g carbs, 6.4g sugars

HAM & PEA PASTIES
If you don't have time to make the pastry, use shop-bought. You could also adapt this recipe to make larger pies or pasties, if you like.
Makes about 24
- ½ tbsp butter
- ½ tbsp olive oil
- 1 leek, finely chopped
- 250g boiled potatoes, finely diced
- 100g peas (frozen is fine)
- 150g cooked ham, diced
- 1 egg, beaten

HAM & PEA PASTIES

CHIPOLATAS WITH MARMALADE GLAZE

Flippin' good

Fritters are a mixture of ingredients bound together with eggs, milk and flour and fried until crisp. The best thing about them is you can use almost any ingredients you fancy, making the humble fritter a brilliant vehicle for those summer vegetable gluts or end-of-week fridge clear-outs. With a little imagination and clever use of spices and flavours, a fritter supper can be a truly beautiful thing. In spring, try fresh garden peas with spring onion and mint, while a cracking summer alternative of grated courgette and sweetcorn makes a super-quick and easy family meal. Of course, fritters don't have to be vegetarian – throw in a handful of shredded cooked chicken or some diced bacon or ham for something more substantial. Then add salad, a zingy tomato and chilli salsa or cool yoghurt based dip on the side and you have a meal worth staying in for.

CORN & CARROT FRITTERS

CHIPOLATAS WITH MARMALADE GLAZE

This easy-to-make snack is an absolute hit at parties. Little effort involved for maximum flavour!
Serves 12
- 2 tsp wholegrain mustard
- 3 tbsp fine-cut marmalade
- 1 tsp olive oil
- 24 good-quality pork chipolatas
- Onion chutney, to serve

1 Preheat the oven to 200C/gas 6. Mix the mustard, marmalade and oil in a bowl. Lay the chipolatas on a baking tray and brush with the glaze. Roast in the oven for 10-12 minutes, basting regularly, until cooked through. Serve with onion chutney.

Per serving 222 cals, 16.2g fat (5.8g saturated), 13.9g protein, 5.1g carbs, 3.5g sugars

CORN & CARROT FRITTERS

A lovely summery lunch or supper. The tzatziki is the perfect cooling partner for the hit of chilli in the fritters.
Makes 6 large fritters
- 200g flour
- 1 tsp baking powder
- 1 tsp ground cumin
- Zest of 1 lime
- 1 red chilli, deseeded and finely diced
- 1 egg
- 200ml milk
- 2 corn cobs, kernels sliced off
- 2 carrots, grated
- 20g butter
Tzatziki
- 100ml yoghurt
- ¼ cucumber, diced
- 1 tbsp chopped mint

1 Combine the flour, baking powder, cumin, lime zest and red chilli in a large bowl. Make a well in the centre, crack in the egg and beat together. Slowly add the milk, drawing in the mixture from the outside of the bowl until you have a nice thick, smooth batter. Stir in the corn kernels and grated carrot, then season with salt and pepper.
2 Heat a little butter in a non-stick pan and spoon in 3 dollops of batter to make 3 fritters. Cook for 4-5 minutes on each side, until lightly golden and the fritters are cooked through. Keep the cooked fritters warm in a clean tea towel.
3 To make the tzatziki, combine the yoghurt, diced cucumber and chopped mint in a bowl, season with black pepper and serve with the warm fritters.

Per serving 257 cals, 6.8g fat (2.8g saturated), 9.3g protein, 42.8g carbs, 7g sugars

CRISPY SWEET POTATO CAKES;
BROAD BEAN, GARLIC & FETA
BRUSCHETTA

Bruschetta, a kind of Italian open sandwich, is a great base for flavour. Instead of the broad bean and feta in the recipe below, try topping with little chunks of super-ripe tomato, tossed in oil with tiny nonpareil capers. For an autumnal variation try meaty strips of field mushroom, fried in butter and chopped parsley

CRISPY SWEET POTATO CAKES

Serves 4
- 600g sweet potatoes, peeled
- 2 medium eggs, whisked
- 50g parmesan, grated
- 1 tbsp Greek yoghurt
- 2 tsp cumin seeds, toasted and ground
- 2–3 tbsp plain flour
- Sunflower oil, for frying
- A handful of chopped mint
- Green salad, to serve (optional)

Sweet chilli dipping sauce
- 150ml Greek yoghurt
- 3 tbsp chilli sauce, ginger sauce, or sweet chilli sauce

1 For the dipping sauce, add the yoghurt to a serving bowl and stir through the chilli or ginger sauce. Set aside.
2 Finely grate the sweet potatoes and squeeze out any moisture. In a large bowl mix the grated sweet potatoes with the eggs, parmesan, yogurt, cumin, seasoning and enough flour to bind.
3 Form the mixture into 8 round patties. Heat the oil in a frying pan and carefully cook the patties for about 4–5 minutes on each side until cooked through.
4 To serve, sprinkle the warm potato cakes with chopped mint, the dipping sauce and green salad on the side.

Per serving 420 cals, 18.6g fat (7.2g saturated), 14g protein, 53.1g carbs, 17.7g sugars

BROAD BEAN, GARLIC & FETA BRUSCHETTA

Serves 6 as a starter
- 1 sourdough loaf
- 300g frozen or fresh broad beans
- A small bunch of tarragon, roughly chopped
- Extra virgin olive oil
- 1 garlic clove
- 4 tbsp fat-free yoghurt
- 100g feta cheese

1 Heat a griddle pan over a high heat until smoking. Cut the bread into 2cm slices and griddle, turning after 1 minute, or when each side has been gently chargrilled. You will need to do this in batches. Set aside.
2 Meanwhile, plunge the beans into a pan of boiling salted water and simmer for 2 minutes, then drain and run under a cold tap until cool. Pop the beans out of their skins, season, stir through the tarragon and gently crush with a fork, so you have a mix of whole and crushed beans. Drizzle with the oil.
3 Halve the garlic cloves and rub onto each slice of griddled bread. In a separate bowl, mash the feta with the yoghurt to form a paste, season and spread thickly onto each garlicky slice, then top with the beans. Drizzle with oil from the bowl.

Per serving 256 cals, 5.9g fat (2.6g saturated), 11.5g protein, 39.5g carbs, 3.3g sugars

GRILLED ASPARAGUS & POACHED EGG ON TOAST

Serves 2
- 2 large slices of good sourdough bread
- Extra virgin olive oil
- 12 asparagus spears
- ½ tsp sweet smoked paprika
- 2 large eggs
- Parmesan, to serve
- 4 sprigs of mint, leaves picked, to serve

1 Bring a pan of salted water to the boil, then reduce to a simmer. Heat a griddle pan over a high heat and toast the bread. Move each slice to a plate or board and drizzle with a little olive oil. Griddle the asparagus for a few minutes on each side, sprinkle with the paprika and divide between the pieces of toast.
2 Poach the eggs in the simmering water for 3 minutes. Remove the eggs with a slotted spoon and drain, then place on top of the asparagus. Grate over the parmesan and sprinkle with mint leaves.

Per serving 278 cals, 11.7 fat (2.6g saturated), 15.8g protein, 25.1g carbs, 2.9g sugars

GRILLED ASPARAGUS & POACHED EGG ON TOAST

magimix®

Built better to last longer

STOP   AUTO   PULSE

Cuisine 5200 XL

magimix

It was in France, in the heart of Burgundy, a region noted for its gastronomy, that Magimix invented the food processor 40 years ago. Magimix products are designed to make life simpler for the serious cook. Most have their roots in professional products designed for commercial use. For this reason they work well and are Built Better to Last Longer. The range combines the best cooking traditions with today's technology, and is supported by strong domestic use guarantees and after sales service. With Magimix, the most demanding tasks can be accomplished quickly, easily and quietly.

www.magimix.com

SOUPS

A good soup is pure comfort in a bowl, and you can make your own using your favourite flavours and ingredients – from fragrant seafood chowders to chunky vegetable broths, the possibilities are endless

SMOKED HADDOCK & PUMPKIN CHOWDER

SMOKED HADDOCK & PUMPKIN CHOWDER

Serves 2

- 200g smoked haddock
- 400ml milk
- A few peppercorns
- 1 bay leaf
- 1 corn on the cob
- 1 onion, roughly chopped
- 1 tbsp olive oil
- 200g pumpkin, peeled and roughly diced
- 1 tbsp saffron, in a little water
- 200ml fish stock
- 100ml double cream
- Sourdough bread, to serve

1 Put the haddock in a pan with the milk, 400ml of water, the peppercorns and bay leaf. Cover and simmer for 10 minutes, until the fish is cooked.
2 Using a sharp knife, carefully slice the kernels from the corn cob. Fry the onion in the olive oil until softened, then add the pumpkin, corn, saffron and fish stock. Season well and cook until the vegetables are softened.
3 Flake the smoked haddock into the pan with the vegetables. Strain the cooking liquor and add enough to the pan to make the soup. Stir in the cream, check the seasoning and serve with slices of fresh sourdough bread.
Per serving 404 cals, 29.9g fat (9.1g saturated), 28.7g protein, 29.4g carbs, 11.4g sugars

CHRISTMAS MULLIGATAWNY SOUP

Give this spicy soup a twist by adding festive leftovers - or anything you like!
Serves 6

- 1 tbsp olive oil
- 1 large onion, sliced
- 1 carrot, sliced
- 2 garlic cloves, sliced
- 1 thumb-sized piece of ginger, grated
- 1 dried red chilli
- 300g butternut squash, cut into 5mm chunks
- 1 tbsp tomato purée
- 1 tbsp curry paste
- 500g leftover roast turkey, shredded
- 1 x 400g tin chopped tomatoes
- 750ml hot chicken or giblet stock
- 300g basmati rice
- ½ small bunch fresh coriander, chopped, to serve

1 Heat the olive oil in a large saucepan over a medium heat, then add the onion, carrot, garlic, ginger and dried chilli. Pop the lid on and cook, stirring occasionally, until all the vegetables are soft, cooked through and lightly golden.
2 Stir in the butternut squash, tomato purée, curry paste and shredded turkey, making sure everything is well coated, then add the chopped tomatoes and season with salt and pepper. Pour in the hot stock and bring to the boil, then reduce to a simmer and cook for 15 minutes. Now add the basmati rice and simmer for a further 10 minutes, until the rice is cooked. Season to taste and serve in big bowls, garnished with the chopped coriander.
Per serving 400 cals, 7.4g fat (1.5g saturated), 32.2g protein, 51.3g carbs, 7.6g sugars

HAM & SPLIT-PEA SOUP

KIPPER CHOWDER

CELERIAC & QUINCE SOUP

Serves 4

- Olive oil
- 1 large celeriac, peeled and chopped
- 1 quince, peeled, cored and chopped
- 2 banana shallots, peeled and chopped
- 2 garlic cloves, chopped
- 1 chicken stock cube, crumbled
- 1 tsp ground cumin
- A pinch of ground cinnamon
- 1 tsp sugar
- 1 tbsp crème fraîche, to serve
- Dill, to serve
- A small handful of walnuts, chopped and toasted in a little butter, to serve

1 Add a generous glug of oil to a large pan and place over a medium-low heat, then add all of the other ingredients. Cook slowly for 20–25 minutes, until the vegetables start to soften, stirring occasionally to make sure nothing catches on the bottom.
2 Pour in enough boiling water to cover the vegetables by 2cm. Pop the lid on and gently simmer for 20–25 minutes, until the vegetables are cooked through. Blitz in a food processor until smooth.
3 Top the soup with a swirl of crème fraîche, a little picked dill and a handful of chopped toasted walnuts.

Per serving 140 cals, 11g fat (2.5g saturated), 3g protein, 6g carbs, 5g sugars

HAM & SPLIT-PEA SOUP

Serves 8–10

- 2 tbsp olive oil, plus extra to serve
- 4 celery stalks, diced
- 2 onions, chopped
- 2 bay leaves
- 2 tbsp chopped thyme
- 1 tsp dried oregano
- 600g yellow split peas, rinsed
- 400g cooked ham
- 1 litre good-quality chicken stock
- Toasted ciabatta, to serve

1 Heat the oil in a saucepan over a medium heat. Add the celery, onions, bay leaves, thyme and oregano, then cook, stirring occasionally, for 8–10 minutes, until the onion is soft.
2 Add the split peas, ham, stock and 1 litre of water; bring to the boil. Reduce the heat to low, cover and simmer for 1 hour or until the split peas are tender.
3 Remove the ham with tongs, transfer to a board and shred with a fork. Mash the split peas in the pan, then stir in the shredded ham. Season to taste, remembering the ham is salty.
4 Gently reheat the soup, if necessary, then stir and ladle into serving bowls. Drizzle with extra olive oil and serve with toasted ciabatta.

Per serving 209 cals, 3.9g fat (1g saturated), 22.1g protein, 20.8g carbs, 6g sugars

KIPPER CHOWDER

Serves 4

- 3 undyed kippers
- 450ml skimmed milk
- 100ml single cream
- 3 sprigs of lemon thyme
- 15g butter
- 1 onion, diced
- 6 slices of pancetta, sliced
- 2 maris piper potatoes, cut into 1cm cubes
- 1 tsp fennel seeds
- A pinch of dried chilli

1 Put the kippers into a saucepan along with the milk and cream and 2 sprigs of lemon thyme. Bring to the boil and simmer for a few minutes. Set aside and leave to infuse.
2 Place a separate saucepan on a medium heat. Add the butter and when it has melted throw in the onion and fry until soft – about 6–8 minutes. Add the pancetta slices, the remaining thyme, the potatoes, fennel seeds and dried chilli. Cook for a few more minutes, then add 250ml of water and the infused milk, setting aside the kippers for later. Cover the saucepan and simmer for 15–20 minutes, or until the potato is cooked, then flake in the kippers and serve.

Per serving 474 cals, 33g fat (10.6g saturated), 27.1g protein, 18.6g carbs, 8.7g sugars

NOVA SCOTIA LOBSTER BISQUE

NOVA SCOTIA LOBSTER BISQUE

A classic bisque is made with lobster broth only, but it's nice to add a bit of the meat for extra flavour and texture.
Recipe by Alain Bosse
Serves 4-6

- 60g butter
- 200g onion, diced
- 100g celery, diced
- ½ carrot, diced
- 1 tbsp chopped fresh thyme
- 1 tbsp chopped fresh parsley
- 3 bay leaves, broken
- 2 whole lobsters, meat removed and cut into chunks (see note)
- 240ml sweet sherry
- 60ml cognac or brandy
- 400ml single cream
- 800ml fish stock
- Crusty bread, to serve

1 Melt the butter in a large saucepan, then fry the onion, celery and carrot over a low heat until softened. Turn down the heat to medium and add the thyme, parsley and bay leaves. Add the lobster shells, which have been separated from the meat (reserve this for later). Simmer gently for about 25 minutes.
2 Add the sherry and cognac and let the mixture reduce until it becomes syrupy. Remove the shells and bay leaves, then purée the liquor in a liquidiser. Once it becomes silky in texture, return it to the saucepan. Over a medium heat, stir in the cream, fish stock and lobster meat and warm through. Serve in big bowls with plenty of crusty bread on the side.
Note Tomalley is the soft green paste found in the body cavity of a lobster – it performs the functions of pancreas and liver. It may not sound enticing but it's considered a delicacy. When preparing cooked lobster, fishmongers will remove it unless you ask for it to be left in.
Per serving 557 cals, 34.4g fat (20.6g saturated), 22.1g protein, 17.3g carbs, 15.2g sugars

ROASTED TOMATO & FENNEL SOUP

Serves 4

- 8 tomatoes
- 1 fennel bulb, cut into 8 wedges, fronds picked
- 1 red chilli, halved lengthways
- 4 garlic cloves
- 2 tbsp olive oil
- A handful of fresh basil
- 150ml chicken or vegetable stock
- Avocado oil, to serve

1 Preheat the oven to 180C/gas 4. Spread out the tomatoes onto a roasting tray and add the fennel wedges, chilli halves and garlic cloves. Toss the vegetables in the oil and season with salt and freshly ground black pepper. Roast for 20 minutes, or until the tomatoes are soft.
2 Transfer the roasted vegetables to a food processor, along with the basil and the stock, and blitz until everything is nice and smooth. Taste for seasoning and add more salt and pepper if required, then serve warm, drizzled with avocado oil and scattered with fennel fronds.
Per serving 105 cals, 7.3g fat (1.1g saturated), 2.7g protein, 7.7g carbs, 6.8g sugars

The Magimix Food Processor is an essential tool to blend soups, such as this roasted tomato and fennel version. But that's not all. Use it to blitz basil leaves with parmesan, pine nuts and olive oil for a pesto to drizzle over the top. You can ring the changes by replacing the basil with rocket or wild garlic. Or go for a red pesto by whizzing charred red pepper with hazelnuts, thyme leaves, garlic and grated pecorino

ROASTED TOMATO & FENNEL SOUP

One machine to rule them all

The multifuctional Food Processor from Magimix is a real flexible friend in the kitchen. It combines simplicity, efficiency and versatility in one handy machine. And it looks great, too, so you'll be more than happy to leave it out on your kitchen work surface.

This useful device is the culmination of Magimix's 40 years of experience producing labour-saving machines. It's simple to use: just three buttons control all functions. It's efficient: the three bowls function independently, so you can carry out several tasks in succession. It's robust, too. The ultra-quiet, commercial-grade motor is covered by a 20-year guarantee, while all parts are covered for 3 years.

But its versatility is where it really comes into its own. A range of attachments are available to enable you to carry out more tasks than ever before. Put it through its paces on the classic gazpacho recipe, opposite, and see for yourself!

CAULIFLOWER & ROASTED GARLIC SOUP

CELERIAC & PEANUT SOUP

This delicious chilled soup couldn't be simpler to prepare, thanks to the Magimix Food Processor. First, skin 6 ripe tomatoes (sit them in boiling water first for a few minutes to loosen their skins). Peel a cucumber, halve it along its length and scrape out the seeds with a teaspoon. Halve a green pepper, discarding the seeds (save the other half for later). And soak 3 slices of stale, good-quality bread in water, then squeeze to remove excess liquid.

All that remains is to add these ingredients to your Magimix Food Processor, along with a roughly chopped onion, and blitz until smooth. Season, then stir through 6 tbsp of good olive oil, 3 tbsp of sherry vinegar and 3 glasses of iced water and you're good to go! An authentic Spanish classic, made in moments.

So whether it's blitzing soups, slicing chopping or dicing fresh veg, puréeing to prepare pestos or houmous, or a host of other uses, Magimix offers maximum functionality in one single stylish machine. For more info and for stockists, log on to Magimix.com or visit Facebook.com/MagimixUK.

CAULIFLOWER & ROASTED GARLIC SOUP

Serves 4

- 1 large garlic bulb, halved horizontally
- 3 tbsp extra-virgin olive oil, plus extra
- 1 onion, chopped
- 1 large cauliflower, cut into florets
- 1.5 litres veg stock
- A few rosemary sprigs, chopped

1 Preheat the oven to 180C/gas 4. Wrap up the garlic and 1 tablespoon of oil in a sheet of foil and roast for 30 minutes.
2 Fry the onion in the remaining oil for 5 minutes, until soft; add the cauliflower for 2 minutes. Pour in the stock, bring to the boil then simmer for 30 minutes.
3 Squeeze the garlic into the soup. Blitz with a food processor until smooth and thin with a little water, if needed. Serve topped with a drizzle of oil, chopped rosemary and black pepper, and bread.
Per serving 160 cals, 11.3g fat (1.6g saturated), 6.9g protein, 7.8g carbs, 4.6g sugars

CELERIAC & PEANUT SOUP

Serves 4

- 1 tbsp olive oil
- 1 onion, diced
- 3 thyme sprigs
- 1 large garlic clove, chopped
- 1 celeriac head, diced
- 1.25 litres vegetable stock
- 125ml single cream
- 100g peanuts, plus extra to serve

1 Heat the oil in a pan and cook the onion, thyme and a pinch of salt for 5-7 minutes, until softened. Add the garlic and celeriac, and cook for 10 minutes.
2 Add the stock, bring to the boil then simmer for 20 minutes, until the celeriac is cooked. Set aside to cool slightly.
3 Blitz in a food processor with the cream and peanuts until smooth. Season and serve with extra peanuts.
Per serving 293 cals, 21.8g fat (6.5g saturated), 12.3g protein, 9.1g carbs, 5.8g sugars

magimix®

Built better to last longer

—— MAKE YOUR ——

PIZZAS

THE

ITALIAN WAY

Adding your own ingredients gives you an opportunity to create flavour combinations that will please the whole family. Mozzarella is a great choice for topping your pizzas and for years Galbani® mozzarella has been the number one choice for Italian & UK families.

Loved for its fresh and delicate milky taste, naturally rich in calcium and free from preservatives, Galbani® mozzarella melts perfectly on your pizza and its stringy consistency will be loved by all.

So make tonight pizza night and make it with Galbani®

PASTA

Whether made from scratch or used dry from the pantry, there's a good reason pasta is on everyone's list of favourites. Cheap, versatile and simple to cook, it's the perfect base for taking on a whole range of different flavours

Nº1 IN ITALIA

Galbani

WILD MUSHROOM STRACCI WITH LEMON & BASIL

ORECCHIETTE WITH YELLOW COURGETTE, PECORINO & CHILLI
Serves 4

- 200g fine semolina flour, plus extra
- 500g yellow courgettes
- Extra virgin olive oil
- 2 garlic cloves, crushed
- 2 dried small red bird's-eye chillies
- A few sprigs of oregano
- A few sprigs of mint
- Aged pecorino, to serve

1 Boil the kettle, then allow to cool for 10 minutes until hot but not boiling. Pour 150ml hot water into a bowl with the flour and mix to a dough, using a knife first then, when cool enough to handle, knead very well with your hands. Generously flour a small wooden board and get yourself a normal dinner knife, preferably with a flexible blade. Tear off small pieces (about the size of chickpeas), flour well and smear across the board with the flat of the knife so they spring up into ear shapes. Place all the orecchiette on a tray dusted with semolina flour and leave to cool and dry.
2 Cut the courgettes into thin wedges, and place in a colander. Sprinkle with a good pinch of salt and leave to sit for half an hour. Rinse with cold running water and pat dry with a tea towel. Set aside.
3 Place a large pan over a medium heat and add a good splash of olive oil. Once hot, add the garlic and crumble in the chillies. Fry for a few seconds, until the garlic turns golden brown, then stir in the oregano. Add the courgettes, season with pepper, and cover. Turn the heat to low and cook for 10-15 minutes, until the courgettes are very soft. Mash gently with a potato masher and keep warm.
4 Cook the pasta in boiling salted water for about 5 minutes (orecchiette rises to the top before it is cooked). Drain, reserving a mug of cooking water.
5 Stir the pasta into the sauce with a splash of olive oil and a little of the pasta water to loosen, if needed. Spoon onto plates, and scatter with chopped mint and grated pecorino. Dust with extra dried chilli if you like a little more bite.
Per serving 215 cals, 2.2g fat (0.2g saturated), 8.5g protein, 38.5g carbs, 2.3g sugars

WILD MUSHROOM STRACCI WITH LEMON & BASIL
Serves 2

- 100g Tipo '00' flour
- 120g fine semolina flour, plus extra
- 1 tbsp powdered porcini mushrooms (see note)
- 2 eggs
- Zest and juice of ½ lemon
- 125ml single cream
- 30g unsalted butter, chopped
- A small bunch of basil, leaves picked, stalks reserved
- Parmesan, to serve

1 In a bowl, mix the flours, powdered mushrooms and eggs to make a dough (it'll be dry, but will come together in the machine). Work it well with your hands, then, using a pasta machine, roll it out onto a surface dusted with semolina flour, not too thin. Cut into random shapes with a crinkly-edged cutter. Dust with semolina flour and lay on a tray.
2 Pop the lemon juice and half the zest in a small saucepan. Add the cream, butter and basil stalks, and place over a medium heat. Stir until the butter dissolves, then take off the heat, and season with salt and pepper. Leave the stalks to infuse for at least 20 minutes.
3 Meanwhile, cook the pasta in a large pan of boiling salted water for 2-3 minutes, until it's all risen to the top.
4 Once the pasta is done, drain and briefly set aside. Warm the sauce gently and pour it through a sieve, pressing the basil stalks to release their flavour. Tip the cooked pasta into the warmed sauce and toss to combine. Spoon into bowls and garnish with more lemon zest, torn basil leaves and grated parmesan.
Note If you can't find any powdered porcini, buy dried mushrooms and grind to a powder with a pestle and mortar.
Per serving 714 cals, 32.4g fat (17.2g saturated), 23g protein, 80.7g carbs, 2.3g sugars

SPICY SICHUAN NOODLES

SPICY SICHUAN NOODLES

Recipe by Ken Hom

"No Chinese New Year meal would be complete without noodles, a symbol of longevity," explains Ken Hom. "As children, we were told never to cut our noodles, lest our lives be cut short. There are many versions of this spicy Sichuan dish, typical of what we Chinese call 'small eats', but I first ate this one at a tiny street restaurant in Chengdu. I have included a vegetarian alternative as an option."

Serves 4

- 225g minced pork or 150g sichuan preserved mustard green stems (see note)
- 3 tbsp low-salt soy sauce
- 225ml groundnut or vegetable oil
- 3 tbsp finely chopped garlic
- 2 tbsp finely chopped ginger
- 5 tbsp finely chopped spring onions
- 2 tbsp sesame paste or peanut butter
- 2 tbsp chilli oil
- 225ml chicken or vegetable stock
- 350g fresh or dried Chinese thin egg noodles
- 1 tbsp Sichuan peppercorns, roasted and ground
- 1 red chilli, deseeded and shredded, to garnish (optional)

1 To make the meat version, combine the pork and 1 tbsp soy sauce in a small bowl, mixing well. Heat a wok or frying pan until hot, then add the oil. Once the oil is hot add the pork and deep-fry, stirring with a spatula to break into small pieces, for 5–6 minutes, or until crispy and dry. Remove with a slotted spoon and drain on kitchen paper. Reserve 2 tablespoons of the oil.
2 For the vegetarian version, rinse the mustard green stems under cold running water, then pat them dry with kitchen paper and chop finely. Note, there's no need for the soy sauce in this version. Stir-fry the greens in the oil for about 3 minutes, then strain over a bowl. Return 2 tablespoons of the oil to the wok.
3 For the sauce, reheat the wok to high and stir-fry the garlic, ginger and spring onions for 30 seconds. Add the sesame paste or peanut butter, chilli oil, stock and remaining 2 tablespoons of soy and 1 teaspoon of salt; simmer for 4 minutes.
4 Meanwhile, cook the noodles in a large pan of boiling water for 2 minutes if fresh; 5 minutes if dried. Drain in a colander, then divide among bowls or transfer to a soup tureen. Ladle on the sauce, top with the pork or greens and ground peppercorns, garnish with chilli, if using, then serve at once.
Note Preserved mustard green stems are available from Asian shops or melburyandappleton.co.uk.
Per serving 630 cals, 30.4g fat (7g saturated), 25.4g protein, 67.9g carbs, 4.4g sugars

CAULIFLOWER & WALNUT TAGLIATELLE

CAULIFLOWER & WALNUT TAGLIATELLE

Serves 4

- 500g cauliflower, or 1 large head, cut into florets
- 350ml chicken stock
- 2 garlic cloves, whole and unpeeled
- 75g butter
- 250g tagliatelle
- 100g walnut halves, roasted
- 75g grated parmesan
- A bunch of flat leaf parsley, chopped

1 Put the cauliflower florets, garlic and butter in a large pan, pour over stock, and season well. Cook over a medium-low heat for 20 minutes, or until the cauliflower is tender.
2 Meanwhile, cook the tagliatelle according to the packet instructions. Drain and return to the pan. Blitz three quarters of the roasted walnuts in a blender, then add the cauliflower and its cooking juices and blitz again. Stir in the parmesan and season to taste.
3 Pour the cauliflower sauce into the pan with the pasta, add the parsley and stir through. Serve the pasta and cauliflower sprinkled with the remaining walnuts and a few sprigs of parsley.
Per serving 684 cals, 41.7g fat (15.1g saturated), 25.2g protein, 54.9g carbs, 7.7g sugars

SINGAPORE NOODLES

SINGAPORE NOODLES

Serves 2

- 1 chicken breast, thinly sliced
- 1 fillet steak, thinly sliced
- 1 tbsp vegetable oil
- 200g raw prawns
- 1 x 400g bag stir-fry vegetables (or chop your own veg)
- 2 x 150g packs of straight-to-wok rice noodles
- A handful of coriander leaves
- 4 spring onions, finely sliced

Sauce

- 3cm piece of root ginger, grated
- 2 garlic cloves, grated
- ½ tbsp sesame oil
- 1 tbsp curry powder
- 3 tbsp soy sauce
- 1 tbsp hoisin sauce
- 1 tbsp sweet chilli sauce

1 Combine the sauce ingredients in a bowl, then add the sliced chicken and steak, mixing to coat well.

2 Place the wok over a medium-high heat and add the oil. Stir-fry the chicken for 5 minutes or until cooked through. Add the steak and prawns, then the veg, still stirring. Pour in the leftover marinade and the noodles, then use 2 forks to toss everything together and keep it moving.

3 When everything is hot and the prawns are pink (about 2 minutes), divide between bowls and scatter over the coriander leaves and spring onions.

Per serving 543 cals, 11.2g fat (2.5g saturated), 34.6g protein, 73.9g carbs, 8.1g sugars

SHRIMP & NOODLE SALAD WITH SWEET CHILLI SAUCE

Rice noodles in stick form just need to be soaked briefly, but you can use any type of rice noodles. The balance of sweet mango, creamy avocado and spicy chilli makes this a brilliantly fresh pick-me-up dish.

Serves 2

- 1 x 100g pack of 3mm rice stick noodles
- 1 small mango, peeled and chopped
- 1 avocado, peeled and chopped
- 100g cooked brown shrimps, peeled
- 1 bunch of coriander cress or coriander, leaves picked

Sweet chilli sauce

- 50g sugar
- 50ml rice wine vinegar
- 1 garlic clove, finely sliced
- 2-3 regular red chillies, deseeded and finely chopped
- 1½ bird's-eye chillies, deseeded and finely chopped

1 For the sauce, pour the sugar, vinegar and 75ml of water into a small pan. Bring to a simmer over a low–medium heat, stirring until the sugar dissolves, then add the garlic and chillies. Simmer for 15 minutes until reduced and syrupy. Set aside to cool.

2 Soak the noodles according to the packet instructions. Drain thoroughly and toss in 3 tbsp of the sweet chilli sauce, adding a little extra, if you like.

3 Add the mango, avocado and shrimps, gently toss everything together, then add the coriander. Serve immediately.

Per serving 536 cals, 15.8g fat (3.3g saturated), 14.7g protein, 79.4g carbs, 36.9g sugars

SHRIMP & NOODLE SALAD
WITH SWEET CHILLI SAUCE

CASARECCE WITH BROCCOLI & ANCHOVIES

CASARECCE WITH BROCCOLI & ANCHOVIES

Recipe by Giorgio Locatelli

If you can't find casarecce pasta, penne is a good substitute.

Serves 4

- 40g breadcrumbs
- 3 salted anchovies (or 6 anchovies in oil)
- 450g broccoli, broken into florets
- 1 tbsp garlic oil
- 4 tbsp olive oil
- 1 garlic clove, peeled and chopped
- 1 fresh red chilli, deseeded and finely chopped
- 50g pine nuts
- 30g sultanas
- 400g casarecce
- 60g each fresh and aged caciocavallo (or pecorino) cheese, grated

1 Toast the breadcrumbs in a dry pan over a medium heat, until they are quite a dark golden brown. Take care not to burn them. If using salted anchovies, rinse and dry them. Run your thumb gently along the backbones to release, and you should pull them out easily. If using anchovies in oil, drain them.
2 Bring a large pan of salted water to the boil and cook the broccoli until just tender. Transfer the broccoli (retaining the cooking water for the pasta) to a bowl of iced water to stop it cooking and keep the bright green colour, then drain and pat dry. Heat the garlic oil in a pan, add the anchovies and stir with a wooden spoon to 'melt' them, taking care not to let them burn. Add the toasted crumbs and set aside.
3 Heat the olive oil in a large pan and add the garlic, chilli and broccoli, and stir until heated through. Season, add the pine nuts and sultanas, and cook for a few more minutes.
4 Meanwhile, bring the broccoli cooking water back to the boil, add the pasta and cook for about a minute less than the time given on the packet. Drain, reserving some of the cooking water, and add to the pan of broccoli, tossing together well for another minute and adding a little cooking water to loosen. Scatter over the two cheeses, the reserved anchovies and the breadcrumbs, and serve.

PASTA & BEANS

Per serving 796 cals, 38.2g fat (9.7g saturated), 29.3g protein, 80.1g carbs, 11g sugars

....

PASTA & BEANS

Recipe by Chris Bianco

This works best with dried beans, but you can use tinned – just double the weight of beans and chickpeas, and sauté them with half the amount of onion, garlic and bay leaves, before mixing with the cooked orecchiette, butter, oregano and parmesan.

Serves 4

- 60g dried cannellini beans
- 60g dried black eyed beans
- 60g dried black pinto beans
- 60g chickpeas
- 2 white onions, halved
- 2 garlic bulbs, peeled and halved
- 4 fresh bay leaves
- 60g dried orecchiette pasta
- 50g butter
- 1 tsp Sicilian oregano, chopped
- 50g parmesan reggiano, grated
- 2 tbsp flat leaf parsley leaves
- Extra virgin olive oil

1 The night before, place each type of bean and the chickpeas in four separate bowls, cover with cold water and leave to soak overnight.
2 The next day, rinse the beans and chickpeas, transfer to a large pan with the onions, garlic and bay leaves, cover with water and bring to the boil. Reduce the heat and simmer for 30-40 minutes, until the beans and chickpeas are tender.
3 Fish out the onions, garlic and bay leaves, bring the beans back to the boil and add the orecchiette. Cook over a medium heat for about 12 minutes, or until the pasta is al dente. Drain and stir in the butter, oregano and parmesan.
4 Serve sprinkled with the torn flat leaf parsley and a drizzle of good olive oil.

Per serving 350 cals, 17.8g fat (9.5g saturated), 16g protein, 27.3g carbs, 2.3g sugars

GLUTEN-FREE FUSILLI WITH ANCHOVIES & SPINACH

Sauce

- 1 red onion, chopped
- 2 celery sticks, chopped
- 30g butter
- Extra virgin olive oil
- 200g chicken livers, trimmed and finely chopped
- 2 sprigs of rosemary, leaves picked and finely chopped
- ½ tsp ground nutmeg
- A good pinch of dried red chilli
- 1 small piece of cassia, or 1 small cinnamon stick
- 1 glass of white wine
- 1 tsp tomato purée
- 200ml tomato passata
- 200ml chicken stock
- 100g fine sourdough breadcrumbs
- Parmesan, grated

1 In a bowl, mix the flours and eggs, then work into a dough using your hands. When it comes together, use a pasta machine to roll it out, not too thin. On a floured surface cut into 1-inch wide strips with a wiggly pasta cutter. Dust with semolina flour and lay on a tray.
2 To make the sauce, blitz the onion and celery in a food processor. Place a large shallow saucepan over a medium heat and add the butter and a splash of oil. Stir in the chicken livers, blitzed veg and half the rosemary. Season with salt and pepper, nutmeg and chilli, then add the cassia. Cook until the moisture evaporates, and the liver and veg begin to caramelise on the base of the pan.
3 Pour in the wine and keep stirring until it evaporates, then stir in the tomato purée. Cook for 1 minute, add the passata and stock, and simmer gently for a further 5 minutes, adding a little water if the sauce gets too dry.
4 Heat a good splash of oil in a large frying pan. Fry the breadcrumbs and remaining rosemary with a little salt and pepper until golden and crisp. Drain on kitchen paper and set aside.
5 Cook the pasta in boiling salted water for 5 minutes, then drain, reserving a little of the pasta water. Stir the pasta into the sauce, loosening with a little cooking water if necessary. Serve piled on a platter, scattered with the rosemary breadcrumbs and grated parmesan.

Per serving 694 cals, 18.9g fat (6.9g saturated), 34.2g protein, 84.8g carbs, 6.1g sugars

GLUTEN-FREE FUSILLI WITH ANCHOVIES & SPINACH

Recipe by Michelle Berriedale-Johnson of freefromrecipesmatter.com
Serves 4

- 4-6 tbsp olive oil
- 1-2 leeks, trimmed and very thinly sliced
- ½ x 50g tin of anchovies
- 100g spinach, roughly chopped
- 300g fresh or dried gluten-free fusilli
- Juice of 1 lemon

1 Heat 2 tablespoons of the olive oil in a wide, heavy pan and add the leeks. Add most of the oil from the tin of anchovies and half of the anchovies, chopped very small with scissors. Cook very gently over a medium heat, uncovered, for 10-15 minutes, or until the leeks are quite soft and the anchovies have melted.

2 Add the chopped spinach to the pan, pop on the lid and let the leaves wilt for 3-4 minutes. Remove from the heat.
3 Meanwhile, cook the fusilli in a pan of salted boiling water according to the packet instructions. Drain, reserving a cup of the cooking water. Return the pasta to the pan, mix in the spinach and leeks and season to taste with salt and freshly ground black pepper. Add a little lemon juice to taste, some of the cooking water to loosen, and a drizzle of olive oil, if needed.

Per serving 410 cals, 14.8g fat (2.2g saturated), 8.3g protein, 60.3g carbs, 2g sugars

SPELT FLOUR PAPPARDELLE WITH CHICKEN LIVER RAGU

Serves 4

- 200g spelt flour
- 200g fine semolina flour, plus extra
- 4 eggs

SPELT FLOUR PAPPARDELLE
WITH CHICKEN LIVER RAGU

The delicate taste of Galbani® fresh mozzarella is great in baked pasta dishes. Add roughly torn strips to a macaroni cheese or between the layers of a lasagne or an aubergine parmigiani to provide pockets of creamy, stringy indulgence. Its soft texture and fresh, milky flavour is perfect in salads, too. Add it to basil and tomato for a classic tricolore, or pair with prosciutto and peaches or with walnuts, figs and rocket for a light, fruity lunch. Ideal with a lively white wine such as sauvignon blanc

SICILIAN MEATBALLS AL FORNO

SICILIAN MEATBALLS AL FORNO

Making meatballs from scratch is a great way of using under-loved, cheap cuts of meat, plus you know exactly what's gone into them. We've kept the pasta simple to let those Sicilian flavours really sing.

Serves 6 (makes 24 meatballs – 4 per person)

- 500g lamb neck fillet and/or offcuts, minced in a food processor
- 100g fresh breadcrumbs
- 50g pine nuts
- Zest of 1 lemon
- 50g raisins, soaked in 3 tbsp balsamic vinegar
- 1 tsp dried oregano
- ½ bunch of flat leaf parsley, leaves picked and finely chopped
- 50g sun-dried tomatoes, chopped
- 50g parmesan cheese, finely grated
- Olive oil
- 120g buffalo mozzarella, torn
- 500g dried spaghetti
- Extra virgin olive oil

Arrabiata sauce

- 1 small red onion, finely chopped
- 2 garlic cloves, finely sliced
- 2 anchovy fillets, chopped
- 1 fresh red chilli, deseeded and finely chopped
- 1 small dried chilli, crumbled
- 800g tinned chopped tomatoes
- A pinch of ground cinnamon
- Red wine vinegar
- 1 tsp sugar (optional)
- ½ bunch of basil, leaves torn

1 Preheat the oven to 200C/gas 6. Put the lamb, breadcrumbs, pine nuts, lemon zest, soaked raisins and their juice, oregano, sun-dried tomatoes, most of the parsley (saving a little to serve) and half the parmesan in a bowl. Season, then mix together well.
2 With wet hands, roll and pat the lamb mixture into 24 meatballs (each one the size of a golf ball). Heat a splash of olive oil in a pan over a high heat, then fry them for about 5 minutes, turning, or until browned all over. Remove from the heat and set aside.
3 For the arrabiata sauce, heat a good glug of olive oil in a pan over a medium heat. Add the onion, garlic, anchovies and chillies, and gently fry for a few

PENNE WITH SPICY SAUSAGE & TOMATO

minutes, until soft. Mix in the chopped tomatoes and cinnamon and simmer over a low heat for about 20 minutes, stirring every so often, or until reduced. Pour in a splash of red wine vinegar, season well, add the sugar if you think it tastes too sharp, and mix through most of the basil leaves.
4 Spoon the sauce into a 25–30cm ovenproof dish, then dot the meatballs over the top, along with the torn pieces of mozzarella. Sprinkle over the remaining basil leaves and parmesan, and bake in the preheated oven for 15–20 minutes, or until golden and bubbling.
5 Meanwhile, cook the spaghetti according to packet instructions, then drain and toss with some extra virgin olive oil and the rest of the parsley. Serve the meatballs with the pasta – perfect with a nice crisp salad.
Per serving 841 cals, 33.3g fat (9.8g saturated), 41.5g protein, 89.7g carbs, 16g sugars

PENNE WITH SPICY SAUSAGE & TOMATO

Serves 4

- 400g dried penne
- 1 onion, chopped
- 4 spicy sausages, chopped
- 1 green chilli, sliced
- 1 tsp fennel seeds
- 14 cherry tomatoes, halved
- Shaved parmesan, to serve

1 Bring a large pan of salted water to the boil and cook the pasta according to the packet instructions.
2 Meanwhile, in a frying pan, heat the oil over a medium heat and cook the onion until softened. Add the sausages, chilli and fennel, and cook for 15 minutes, stirring frequently. Add the tomatoes and cook until softened.
3 Drain the pasta and toss the sausage mix through it. Serve with the parmesan.
Per serving 477 cals, 17.1g fat (5.3g saturated), 19.2g protein, 66.1g carbs, 7.2g sugars

Perfect pasta

Delicately creamy Galbani® Ricotta enrobes slivers of tagliatelle pasta in this simple midweek supper dish. Just before serving, sprinkle over a good grinding of Galbani® Grana Padano to enhance its savoury depth.

TAGLIATELLE WITH RICOTTA
Serves 4

- 1 onion, finely chopped
- Olive oil
- A handful of garden peas, boiled
- A bay leaf
- 500g Tagliatelle
- 200g Galbani® Ricotta
- Black olives
- A couple of sprigs of thyme, leaves only
- Galbani® Grana Padano, freshly grated, to serve
- Rocket or basil pesto, to serve

Sauté the onion in a little olive oil with the peas and the bay leaf. Cook the pasta according to the packet directions. Drain and stir in a little olive oil, add the ricotta, olives, onion and peas. Season with black pepper, sprinkle with the thyme and serve with freshly grated grana padano and a spoonful of pesto.

MAC & CHEESE

Want to indulge in your favourite comfort dish but with less guilt? This recipe is lower in fat than regular versions of this dish, thanks to the low-fat cottage cheese, while the mature cheddar and the parmesan ensure you still get that hit of creamy, cheesy flavour.

Serves 6

- 400g macaroni, or other pasta
- 1 tsp butter
- 2 garlic cloves, finely chopped
- 200g spinach
- 3 tbsp flour
- 150ml semi-skimmed milk
- 2 bay leaves
- 400g low-fat cottage cheese
- 75g strong mature cheddar, grated
- 50g parmesan, grated

1 Preheat the oven to 190C/gas 5. Cook the pasta in a large pan of salted boiling water according to packet instructions, but for 2 minutes less than it says, so the pasta is al dente. Drain, reserving a little of the cooking water, and set aside.
2 Meanwhile, melt the butter in a pan over a medium heat. Add the garlic and cook for about 1 minute, then add the spinach and 1 tablespoon of water. Reduce the heat, cover with a lid and cook for about 5 minutes, or until the spinach has wilted. Drain, pressing out any excess liquid, and set aside.
3 In a separate pan, gradually whisk the flour into the milk over a low heat until you have a smooth sauce. Add the bay leaves and a pinch of black pepper and bring to the boil, whisking continuously. Reduce the heat and simmer for a couple of minutes, stirring, until the sauce has thickened. Remove the pan from the heat and discard the bay leaves.
4 Tip the cottage cheese into a bowl and blitz with a stick blender until smooth, then gradually stir into the milk sauce, along with most of the cheddar and half of the parmesan, until combined.
5 Stir the pasta through the cheese sauce, adding a little of the reserved water to loosen, if needed. Mix in the spinach, tip into a 20 x 26cm baking dish and top with the remaining cheeses. Bake for 30-35 minutes until golden.
Per serving 449 cals, 10.9g fat (6.1g saturated), 27.1g protein, 59.5g carbs, 4g sugars

3-PEA SPAGHETTI

(not pictured)
Serves 2

- 200g spaghetti
- 2 tbsp olive oil
- 100g each sugar snaps, petit pois and mange tout
- 2 garlic cloves, sliced
- Juice and zest of ½ lemon
- 100g feta, crumbled
- 2 tbsp chopped mint

1 Cook the spaghetti according to packet instructions. Heat the oil in a frying pan over a medium heat and cook all three types of peas for about 3 minutes, stirring regularly. Add the garlic and cook for 1 minute more.
2 Remove from the heat, stir through the lemon juice, feta, mint and zest. Drain the spaghetti and toss through the pea mixture. Season with black pepper.
Per serving 666 cals, 25.9g fat (9.2g saturated), 27.2g protein, 86.4g carbs, 9.1g sugars

DUCK RAGU PAPPARDELLE

(not pictured)
Serves 6

- 700g duck meat (breast and leg), diced
- 1 tbsp olive oil
- 2 onions, chopped
- 2 carrots, chopped
- 2 celery stalks, chopped
- 2 garlic cloves, chopped
- 1 bay leaf
- A handful of thyme stalks
- 350ml red wine
- 2 tbsp tomato purée
- 2 tsp paprika
- 500g pappardelle pasta

1 Preheat the oven to 170C/gas 3 and season the duck. In a casserole, heat the oil and brown the meat over a medium heat. Add the veg and garlic, and cook until golden. Tuck in the bay and thyme, pour in the wine, stir in the tomato purée and paprika and season.
2 Cover and cook in the oven for 1½ hours, checking often. 10 minutes before serving, cook the pappardelle according to the pack instructions and drain. Stir the duck ragù through the pasta.
Per serving 617 cals, 15.1g fat (3.3g saturated), 43.5g protein, 71.2g carbs, 9.7g sugars

Divine dessert

The silky texture of Galbani® Mascarpone brings a luxurious richness to this summer-berry take on a classic Italian pudding.

RASPBERRY TIRAMISU
Serves 4

- 3 eggs, separated
- 50g sugar
- 250g Galbani® Mascarpone
- 200g sponge fingers
- 1 large glass fruit juice (orange or tropical fruit)
- 1 tbsp marsala or Cointreau (optional)
- 200g raspberries
- A few mint leaves, shredded, to serve

In a bowl, beat together the egg yolks and sugar until pale and thick. Stir in the mascarpone. In another bowl, whisk the egg whites until stiff peaks form and fold into the mascarpone mixture. Dip half of the sponge fingers in the fruit juice (to which you can add the marsala or Cointreau, if desired), arrange them on a dish and cover with half of the mascarpone cream. Create another layer of soaked sponge fingers and cover this with the remaining mascarpone cream. Chill for at least 4 hours. Decorate with the raspberries and strew over the mint before serving.

CHRISTMAS CARBONARA

CHRISTMAS CARBONARA

Serves 4

- 400g dried tagliatelle, or other pasta
- 150g mushrooms, sliced
- 1 garlic clove, finely chopped
- 1 tbsp olive oil
- 2 egg yolks
- 100g crème fraîche
- 50g parmesan, grated, plus extra to serve (optional)
- 1 tbsp finely chopped flat-leaf parsley
- 1 tbsp finely chopped chives
- 80g cooked ham, shredded

1 Cook the tagliatelle in a large pan of salted boiling water until al dente.
2 Meanwhile, in a frying pan, soften the mushrooms and garlic in the oil over a medium heat for 5 minutes.
3 In a bowl, beat together the egg yolks, crème fraîche, parmesan, parsley and chives. Season well with black pepper. Stir in the fried mushrooms and ham.
4 Drain the tagliatelle, saving a cupful of the cooking water, then return it to the pan. Off the heat, pour the sauce over the pasta and stir to coat. Add some cooking water to loosen, if needed. Serve with extra grated parmesan, if you like.

Per serving 585 cals, 20g fat (10g saturated), 25.5g protein, 75.5g carbs, 5.1g sugars

WHOLEWHEAT RAVIOLI WITH COURGETTE FLOWERS & RICOTTA

WHOLEWHEAT RAVIOLI WITH COURGETTE FLOWERS & RICOTTA

Serves 4

- 200g Tipo '00' flour, plus extra
- 100g wholewheat flour
- 3 eggs

Filling
- 20 courgette flowers
- 250g good-quality ricotta
- A few sprigs of mint, leaves picked and finely chopped
- 1 small red chilli, finely chopped

Sauce
- 600g ripe tomatoes
- A small bunch of basil, leaves picked, stalks reserved
- Extra virgin olive oil
- Young pecorino, grated, to serve

1 In a bowl, mix the flours and eggs and work to a soft dough with your hands.

When it comes together, using a pasta machine roll the pasta out thinly and evenly and place on a surface well-floured with Tipo '00' flour. Set aside.
2 Pick the soft yellow parts of the courgette flowers and chop finely, taking care not to crush them. Add to a bowl with the ricotta, mint and chilli. Season, mix well and spoon into a piping bag with a 1cm nozzle. Pipe teaspoon-sized blobs in a line on the bottom half of the pasta sheet, 3-4cm apart.
3 Brush the edges around the filling with a little water, fold the top half of the pasta down onto the half with the filling. Squeeze out any air and press to seal the edges. With a crinkly pasta cutter, trim into separate ravioli and place on a tray well-floured with Tipo '00' flour.
4 To make the sauce, halve the tomatoes and squeeze the seeds into a sieve over a bowl. Put the tomato halves cut-side down in a wide saucepan and add the juice from the seeds. Discard the seeds.

5 Add enough water to the pan to come half way up the sides of the tomatoes, and season well. Add the basil stalks, cover and bring to the boil over a high heat. Turn the heat down and cook for 1-2 minutes. Remove the lid and pinch the skins from the tomatoes with a pair of tongs. Discard the skins, then mash the tomatoes with a potato masher. Cook, stirring occasionally, until reduced. Fish out the basil stalks and discard. Tear up most of the basil leaves and add to the pan with a good splash of olive oil.
6 Cook the ravioli in plenty of boiling salted water for 5 minutes, until risen to the top, then use a slotted spoon to transfer them to the pan of tomato sauce. Gently turn the pasta to coat in the sauce and leave for a minute for the pasta to absorb some of it. Spoon the ravioli onto 4 plates and top with some basil leaves and grated pecorino.

Per serving 465 cals, 14.7g fat (6.3g saturated), 21.8g protein, 58.6g carbs, 9.9g sugars

Created just for you

Enjoy the real flavour of India
with my delicious range of authentic
chutneys, pickles, sauces and pastes
made with the finest ingredients and
a whole lot of love and know~how.

Geeta Samtani

Geeta's®
The Real Flavour of India

Check out our full range and find out more at **geetasfoods.com**

Available at most leading supermarkets

RICE

This mighty little grain is one of the most versatile foods around – enjoy it as the main component of your meal, a side, or even in a dessert. Thousands of different varieties of the grain exist so start experimenting!

Geeta's®

The Real Flavour of India

COCONUT RICE & PEAS

STEAMED VIETNAMESE STICKY RICE PARCELS

COCONUT RICE & PEAS
Serves 8
- 300g dried red kidney beans
- 1 small bunch of fresh thyme
- 2 garlic cloves, crushed
- 2 spring onions, bashed
- 6 allspice berries
- 1 cinnamon stick
- 1 x 400ml tin reduced fat coconut milk
- 325g basmati rice

1 Wash the kidney beans and soak overnight in plenty of cold water.
2 Drain the beans and bring to the boil in a large pan with 2 litres of cold water, the thyme, garlic, spring onions, allspice and cinnamon. Simmer for 1 hour, until tender.
3 Transfer the beans to a clean pan with 600ml of the cooking liquid and the coconut milk. Bring to a simmer and cook for 5 minutes. Add the rice and cook for a further 15-20 minutes, until tender. Season to taste and serve immediately.
Per serving 286 cals, 4.3g fat (3.2g saturated), 12.2g protein, 46g carbs, 1.5g sugars,

STEAMED VIETNAMESE STICKY RICE PARCELS
Serves 4-6
- 2 green tea with jasmine teabags
- 125g sticky rice
- 125ml coconut milk
- 60g caster sugar
- 35g roasted salted peanuts, chopped
- A few banana leaves
- 1 banana, sliced

1 Brew the tea bags in a bowl with plenty of hot water for 5 minutes, then discard the bags and tip in the rice. Leave to soak for several hours, or overnight.
2 Rinse the rice, then steam in a baking paper-lined sieve or colander for about 25 minutes, or until tender. Meanwhile, in a pan, simmer the coconut milk with the sugar over a medium heat for about 5 minutes. Combine the rice and coconut, then stir through the chopped peanuts.
3 Cut the banana leaves into 20-25cm long pieces, then cook in a pan of boiling water for 5-10 minutes, or until pliable. Shake dry, then pile the rice onto 4-6 pieces of banana leaf, adding banana slices as you go. Wrap up tightly, then lie, seam-side down, in a colander and steam for 25-30 minutes, or until the leaves are drier, and the parcels feel quite firm. Eat warm or at room temperature.
Per serving 312 cals, 9.6g fat (5.1g saturated), 5.5g protein, 52.4g carbs, 26.2g sugars

TACU TACU
Serves 4
- 300g long-grain white rice
- 1 plantain, peeled
- Olive oil
- 2 garlic cloves, chopped
- 1 onion, finely chopped
- 1 red chilli, finely sliced
- Hot chilli sauce (Cholula is great)
- 1 x 400g tin of haricot beans, drained
- 4 eggs

1 Cook the rice according to packet instructions, then drain and leave to cool.
2 Slice the plantain about 1.5cm thick. In a non-stick frying pan over a medium heat, fry the plantain in a couple of glugs of oil for a few minutes on each side, until golden. Set aside and keep warm.
3 In the same pan, fry the garlic, onion and chilli over a medium-low heat for 5-10 minutes, or until soft and lightly golden. Stir in 1 tablespoon of hot chilli sauce; add the beans and cooled rice.
4 Turn the heat up to high and fry the until the rice is beginning to crisp, stirring regularly. Stop stirring for the last couple of minutes to let it get golden and crisp on the bottom – this is your tacu tacu! Transfer to a plate; set aside.
5 Add a little more oil to the same pan and fry the eggs, adding the plantain for the last minute to warm through.
6 Serve the tacu tacu portions topped with a fried egg, some crispy plantain and a dash more chilli sauce, if you like.
Per serving 476 cals, 10.8g fat (2.1g saturated), 18.4g protein, 74.8g carbs, 9.9g sugars

TACU TACU

HAM & STILTON RISOTTO

KEDGEREE

BIRYANI

HAM & STILTON RISOTTO

Serves 4-6

- 750ml good-quality chicken or vegetable stock
- 1 onion, finely diced
- 30g unsalted butter, plus a knob extra
- 500g risotto rice
- 200ml dry white wine
- 100g stilton
- 200g cooked ham, thinly shredded

1 In a saucepan over a medium heat, bring the stock and 750ml water up to a simmer, then leave on the heat.
2 In a large, heavy-based pan gently fry the onion in the butter over a low heat for 10-12 minutes, until softened.
3 Turn up the heat, tip in the risotto rice and cook, stirring, for a minute or so, until the rice is slightly translucent. Add the wine and continue to stir until all of the liquid is absorbed.
4 Stir in a ladleful of the warm stock and reduce the heat to a simmer. Continue stirring in the stock, a ladleful at a time, making sure each one is absorbed before adding the next. After 15-20 minutes, taste the rice – it should be al dente. If not, add a little more stock or hot water.
5 Stir in most of the stilton until it begins to melt into the risotto. Take the pan off the heat and stir in most of the ham and a knob of butter. Cover and leave to stand

for 2 minutes. Season to taste and serve with the remaining ham and stilton.

Per serving 855 cals, 23.1g fat (13.2g saturated), 32.2g protein, 120.7g carbs, 6.7g sugars

....

KEDGEREE

Serves 4

- 2 tbsp olive oil
- 1 onion, sliced
- 1 tsp sumac
- 1½ tsp ground cumin
- 1 cinnamon stick
- 1 bay leaf
- 220g rice (wild or long grain)
- 300ml vegetable stock
- 2 medium eggs
- 2 undyed kippers
- 2 tbsp pomegranate seeds, to serve
- 2 tbsp chopped parsley, to serve

1 Heat the oil in a pan and fry the onion for 5-7 minutes, until soft. Add the spices and bay leaf and cook for a few more minutes, then add the rice, stock and 300ml of water. Simmer for 25 minutes, until the rice is cooked.
2 Meanwhile, boil the eggs for 6 minutes, then plunge into cold water to cool. Peel and cut each egg into six wedges.
3 Grill the kippers under a medium heat for 5 minutes, then flake off the flesh and stir through the rice mixture. Serve immediately, sprinkled with the

pomegranate seeds and parsley.

Per serving 482 cals, 22.8g fat (3.7g saturated), 21.4g protein, 48.3g carbs, 3.2g sugars

....

BIRYANI

Serves 4

- 750g cooked and cooled basmati rice (about 200g uncooked weight)
- A small bunch of mint, leaves picked
- About 600g leftover chicken curry (on the bone if you want to be authentic)
- 25g butter, melted
- A few sprigs of coriander, to serve
- Chappatis, chutney and yoghurt, to serve (optional)

1 Preheat the oven to 200C/gas 6. Spread out half the cooked rice in the base of a 23cm round ovenproof dish and dot with half of the mint leaves, then spread the curry over the top.
2 Dot with the remaining mint and top with the rest of the rice. Drizzle over the melted butter and cover with a lid or foil.
3 Bake for 25-30 minutes, or until steaming hot throughout, then remove the lid/foil and finish in the oven for a further 10 minutes, until few of the grains of rice begin to crisp up. Top with the coriander and serve with chappatis, chutney and yoghurt, if you like.

Per serving 393 cals, 11.2g fat (3.7g saturated), 23.3g protein, 47g carbs, 3.5g sugars

KHICHDI

3 Add the greens and a splash more boiling water if needed. Cook for a further 5-10 minutes and serve.

Per serving 366 cals, 11.1g fat (6.7g saturated), 11.8g protein, 51g carbs, 2.8g sugars

....

PORK & CLAMS CATAPLANA

This Portuguese classic is traditionally cooked in a two-sided wok-style 'cataplana' that clips together to steam the ingredients to perfection.

Serves 6–8
- 500g pork leg or shoulder, cut into 1cm cubes
- Olive oil for frying
- 1½ tbsp pimento paste
- 1 fresh bay leaf
- 350ml white wine or vinho verde
- 300g long grain rice
- 500g clams, rinsed

Marinade
- 2 tbsp olive oil
- 2 tbsp red wine vinegar
- 2 garlic cloves, roughly chopped
- ½ tbsp dried oregano

1 Combine all the marinade ingredients in a large bowl and season. Add the diced pork and leave in the fridge to marinate for at least an hour but up to 24 hours.
2 Fry the marinated pork over a medium heat in 1 tablespoon of olive oil for about 5 minutes, or until browned all over. Add the pimento paste and bay leaf, stir well and cook for 8-10 minutes. Turn the heat down to low-medium, add the wine and simmer for 45-60 minutes, or until tender. If the mixture becomes too dry, add a little extra water to loosen it.
3 In another pan, cook the rice in 500ml of salted water over a low-medium heat until just tender, then drain. Add the rice to the pork with a cup of boiling water and stir everything together gently - the mixture should be juicy and saucy.
4 Scatter the clams on top and put a lid on the pan. Cook over a medium-high heat for 5-10 minutes, until the clams have opened, discarding any that remain closed. Season and serve.

Per serving 472 cals, 20.3g fat (5.3g saturated), 24.2 g protein, 38.5g carbs, 0.9g sugars

KHICHDI

This comforting South Asian rice dish harmoniously combines spices for a gentle yet moreish flavour. As with any rice dish, be careful about storing and reheating any leftovers - make sure it's piping hot all the way through. Of course you're unlikely to have any leftovers with this recipe!

Serves 6 or 10-12 as a side
- 3 tbsp ghee (or olive oil)
- ½ tbsp cumin seeds
- 300g basmati rice
- 150g split mung beans, washed
- 3 garlic cloves, sliced
- 2 onions, finely chopped
- 1 green chilli, deseeded and finely sliced
- 15 curry leaves
- 2cm piece of ginger
- 1 tsp mustard seeds
- 1 tsp ground turmeric
- 1 small cinnamon stick
- 200g kale or spinach, roughly chopped

1 Heat a little of the ghee in a large saucepan over a medium heat and add the cumin seeds. Once they start to turn golden and release their aroma, add the rice and mung beans to the saucepan, season well with salt and pepper and add 175ml of water. Bring to the boil, then reduce to a simmer, cover and cook for around 45 minutes.
2 While the rice and mung beans are cooking you can temper the rest of the spices. To do this, heat the rest of the ghee in a frying pan over a medium heat and add the garlic. Once the garlic has turned golden, add the onion, chilli and curry leaves and grate in the ginger. Sauté for 5-10 minutes until the onion has softened but not coloured. Turn up the heat a little and add the mustard seeds, turmeric and cinnamon stick. Fry quickly for 1-2 minutes, then stir through the rice and mung beans when they are ready. Cover and cook for a further 15 minutes.

Portuguese cataplana is one of several dishes worldwide to mix seafood, meat and rice. In Spain, paella combines seafood with strips of chicken and chunks of chorizo, while Chinese fried rice mixes rice with egg, pork or chicken and prawns (its Indonesian cousin, nasi goreng, omits the pork). In Korean bibimbap, meanwhile, steamed white rice is topped with sautéed veg, sliced meat and a fried egg

PORK & CLAMS CATAPLANA

Rice, rice, baby

Basic risotto is a great recipe to get creative with. Add anything you like to make it your own, whether it's smoked chicken, pancetta, asparagus, peas, prawns or goat's cheese. Risotto is also great for arancini: mould a ball of risotto around some mozzarella, dip in beaten egg, flour, then breadcrumbs, and shallow fry in hot oil, turning until golden all over.

TOMATO, RED WINE & CHORIZO RISOTTO

BASIC RISOTTO

Serves 6

- 1.5 litres of chicken stock
- Extra virgin olive oil
- 1 onion, finely chopped
- 1 garlic clove, finely chopped
- 1 stick of celery, trimmed and finely chopped
- A small bunch of thyme, leaves picked
- 450g risotto rice
- 2 glasses of white wine (about 350ml)
- 75g peas
- Zest of 1 lemon
- 20g parmesan, grated
- A knob of butter

1 Heat the stock in a saucepan over a medium heat, bring to the boil and turn down to a low simmer.
2 Place a large, deep frying pan over a medium heat, add a little olive oil and fry the onion, garlic, celery and thyme for 5-10 minutes, until softened but not coloured. Tip in the rice and fry for a minute until the grains are slightly translucent. Pour in the wine and stir continuously until it evaporates.
3 Add a ladleful of stock, stir constantly until it has reduced by three-quarters, then add another ladleful. Keep doing this until the rice has absorbed most or all of the stock, but is slightly al dente.
4 Stir through the peas and half the lemon zest, most of the parmesan and the butter. Turn off the heat, pop the lid on and rest for a few minutes. Taste and season. Serve with some more parmesan, as much of the remaining lemon zest as you fancy, and a drizzle of olive oil.
Per serving 401 cals, 5.8g fat (3g saturated), 14g protein, 63.1g carbs, 2.4g sugars

TOMATO, RED WINE & CHORIZO RISOTTO

Serves 4

- 2 tbsp olive oil
- 2 shallots, finely chopped
- 1 garlic clove, finely chopped
- 80g chorizo, finely chopped
- A small bunch of flat leaf parsley, leaves picked, stalks finely chopped
- 750ml-1 litre chicken or veg stock
- 1 x 400g tin chopped tomatoes
- 300g risotto rice
- 200ml red wine
- 50g parmesan, grated, plus extra to serve

1 Heat the oil in a wide, shallow pan and add the shallots, garlic, chorizo and parsley stalks (reserve the leaves to serve). Cook over a medium-high heat for 5 minutes, or until the shallot is softened and the chorizo is beginning to go crisp.
2 Meanwhile, in another pan, heat the stock with the tinned tomatoes. Add the rice to the shallot mixture and stir to coat the grains. Cook over a high heat for a minute or two, or until the grains have cracked and are slightly translucent at the tips, then pour in the red wine. Stir well and cook until almost all the wine has evaporated.
3 Add the hot stock and tomato mixture, ladle by ladle, stirring well with each addition, and only adding more when the previous ladle is almost fully absorbed. You may not need all of the mixture, or you may need to top it up with a little water. The rice should be tender but with a little bite in the middle. When it's cooked, add one last ladle of liquid, along with the parmesan and some seasoning.
4 Stir well, take off the heat and cover. Leave for 5 minutes before stirring again. Taste and adjust the seasoning if necessary. Serve topped with extra parmesan and chopped parsley leaves.
Per serving 504 cals, 16.5g fat (5.3g saturated), 17g protein, 63.1g carbs, 4.1g sugars

NO-ONE PUTS TENDERSTEM®

in the corner

Tenderstem®
broccoli

my goodness

Try our French-inspired warm Tenderstem® salad with roasted Camembert, croutons and shallot vinaigrette. Plus, discover more from around the world that you can deliver to your table in just 10 minutes.

around the world with Tenderstem® in 10

win a cooking class

www.tenderstem.co.uk

SALAD & VEG

Packed with good things, cost-effective,
and absolutely delicious – veggies are the
stars of the food world. From superior salads
to hearty hot mains, there really is a root,
leaf and legume for every occasion

EPIC EGG SALAD

among the eggs, drizzling over a little of the anchovy marinade, too. Serve with the salad cream on the side – so simple, so delicious.

Per serving 332 cals, 30.1g fat (3.7g saturated), 9.6g protein, 4.2g carbs, 2.9g sugars

STILTON & SPROUTING BROCCOLI FRITTATA

Serves 4

- 200g purple sprouting broccoli, florets cut from stalks, stalks sliced
- Extra virgin olive oil
- 6 eggs
- 1 small bunch of flat leaf parsley, leaves picked, stalks finely sliced
- 50g stilton, or other blue cheese, crumbled
- 1 heaped tbsp freshly grated parmesan cheese
- A knob of unsalted butter

Salad
- 25g pine nuts
- 1 lemon

1 Preheat the oven to 220C/gas 7 and heat a griddle pan. Blanch the broccoli stalk pieces in boiling salted water for 1–2 minutes, then drain. Toss with the florets in a little olive oil, then griddle over a high heat for 8–10 minutes, or until charred and just tender. Leave to cool in a bowl, drizzling a little more oil.
2 In a bowl, whisk the eggs, season with salt and pepper, then stir in the parsley stalks, cheeses and broccoli.
3 Melt the butter with a little oil in a shallow 20cm ovenproof pan over a medium heat. Pour in the egg mixture, quickly stir a few times to let the egg settle, then cook for 2–3 minutes, or until it starts to set.
4 Pop the pan in the oven for about 8–10 minutes, or until the frittata is puffed up, golden and completely set.
5 Meanwhile, make the salad. Toast the pine nuts in a dry pan over a medium heat, moving them frequently, until golden all over. In a serving bowl, toss the parsley leaves and toasted nuts in a splash of extra virgin olive oil and a squeeze of lemon juice. Then take your gorgeous frittata out of the oven and serve immediately with the salad.

Per serving 380 cals, 33.2g fat (9.6g saturated), 16.9g protein, 2.1g carbs, 1.5g sugars

EPIC EGG SALAD

When done properly, egg salads are out of this world. Homemade salad cream makes this dish top notch.

Serves 4

- 4 anchovies in olive oil, halved lengthways, reserving 1 tbsp of the oil
- Finely grated zest and juice of ½ lemon
- A small bunch of flat leaf parsley, finely chopped
- A small bunch of chives, finely chopped
- 4 eggs
- 2 round lettuces, smaller leaves picked
- 1 red chicory, base finely sliced, leaves separated
- 1 white chicory, base finely sliced, leaves separated
- 1 x 20g punnet of cress

Salad cream
- ½ garlic clove, crushed
- 2 tsp dijon mustard
- 2 tbsp cider vinegar
- 6 tbsp rapeseed oil
- 3 tbsp buttermilk

Chilli salt
- 1 dried red chilli
- 3 tbsp sea salt

1 Marinate the anchovies in a bowl with the reserved tablespoon of oil, lemon zest and juice, and a little of the parsley and chives.
2 In a bowl, whisk together all of the salad cream ingredients, then season to taste and set aside.
3 To make the chilli salt bash the chilli and salt together using a pestle and mortar. Set aside.
4 Boil the eggs in salted water for about 6 minutes, then refresh in cold water until cool enough to handle. Peel the eggs and set aside.
5 Arrange the lettuce leaves and chicory on a serving platter. Scatter over the remaining chopped parsley and chives, snip over the cress, then halve the eggs and place on top. Sprinkle over some chilli salt and divide the anchovies

Aubergine is something we're a bit wary of in the UK. Shame, because it can be easy to use. Simply prick the fruit several times, put in a hot oven and bake till soft. When cool, scoop out the flesh and add chopped garlic, parsley, olive oil and lemon juice for aubergine caviar. For a Levantine variant, add tahini and it becomes baba ganoush. Or stuff the aubergine caviar back into the fruit's skins with feta and minced lamb and bake

VIETNAMESE GRIDDLED AUBERGINE SALAD

COLD SESAME BROCCOLI

SALAD WEDGES WITH BUTTERMILK DRESSING

VIETNAMESE GRIDDLED AUBERGINE SALAD

Serves 2

- 1 tbsp jasmine rice
- 2 small aubergines, sliced 3mm thick
- 1 tbsp groundnut oil
- 3 spring onions, finely sliced
- 75g beansprouts, blanched and refreshed
- 1 red chilli, finely sliced
- A handful of mint leaves
- 1 x 30g punnet of micro garlic chives
- 1 tbsp roasted salted peanuts, chopped

Dressing

- 1 tbsp fish sauce
- 1 tsp tamarind paste
- 1 tsp palm sugar

1 To make the dressing heat all the ingredients in a small pan over a medium heat for 3-5 minutes, stirring, until the sugar has dissolved. Set aside to cool.
2 Toast the rice in a dry frying pan over a medium heat for 8-10 minutes, shaking occasionally, until golden and crisp. Using a pestle and mortar, grind to a coarse powder, then set aside.
3 Heat a griddle pan until searing, brush the aubergine with the oil and char for 3 minutes on each side until tender.
4 Divide the aubergine between 2 plates, scatter over the spring onions, beansprouts, chilli, mint and micro garlic chives, and drizzle with the dressing. Finish with a scattering of the chopped peanuts and the toasted rice powder.

Per serving 261 cals, 10.8g fat (2.1g saturated), 6.7g protein, 29.6g carbs, 20.7g sugars

....

COLD SESAME BROCCOLI

Recipe by Ken Hom

Serves 4-6

- 650g broccoli
- 1 tbsp sesame seeds
- 1 tbsp groundnut or vegetable oil
- 2 tsp sesame oil
- 2 tsp finely chopped garlic
- 1½ tbsp light soy sauce
- 2 tbsp finely chopped spring onion

1 Preheat the oven to 190C/gas 5 or turn on the grill. Cut off the broccoli florets; peel and slice the stems. Blanch in salted boiling water for 4-5 minutes; refresh in cold water. Drain and place in a bowl.
2 Roast the sesame seeds in the oven or under the grill until brown. In a bowl, mix the sesame seeds with the remaining ingredients. Pour over the broccoli and toss to coat. You can make this the day before and chill until needed; cover with cling film and let the broccoli come to room temperature before serving.

Per serving 125 cals, 7.1g fat (1.3g saturated), 8.3g protein, 4.2g carbs, 2.8g sugars

SALAD WEDGES WITH BUTTERMILK DRESSING

Serves 8

- 75g almonds
- A handful of mixed seeds
- 125g sugar
- 1 iceberg lettuce, cut into wedges
- 4 little gem lettuces, cut into wedges
- 4 endives
- 150ml buttermilk
- Zest of 2 lemons, juice of 1
- Extra virgin olive oil
- A bunch of chives, finely chopped

1 Toast the almonds in a dry non-stick frying pan until golden, then add the seeds. Sprinkle in the sugar and a pinch of salt and heat until the sugar dissolves. Gently swirl the pan until you have a golden caramel, then pour onto a greaseproof-lined tray. Set aside to cool.
2 Meanwhile, arrange the lettuces and endives on a platter and set aside.
3 Spoon the buttermilk into a jar, season and add the lemon zest, juice and a couple of spoonfuls of extra virgin olive oil. Shake well and set aside.
4 Crush the caramelised nuts and seeds with a pestle and mortar to a mixture of fine and chunky. Dress the salad; scatter over the chives and nuts and seeds.

Per serving 206 cals, 10.5g fat (1.2g saturated), 5.7g protein, 19.9g carbs, 19.2g sugars

evaporated and the pork is tender, cooked and starting to crisp up again.
4 In a separate pan, heat the rest of the groundnut oil. Add the cube of bread; if it browns in 10 seconds, your oil is hot enough to start frying. In batches, fry the basil leaves for 3 seconds, until they're translucent and crisp (careful of the hot oil, as it may spit). Remove the crispy leaves with a slotted spoon and set aside to dry on kitchen paper.
5 To serve, place the lettuce leaves on a serving plate, scatter over the pork, pickled carrots, reserved spring onion and crispy basil leaves. Drizzle with a little of the carrots' pickling liquid and serve immediately.

Note Holy basil is a spicy herb similar to both mint and basil. You can get it online at thai-food-online.co.uk, or just substitute regular basil.

Per serving 467 cals, 25g fat (7.5g saturated), 35.1g protein, 22.2g carbs, 16.4g sugars

CRISPY BASIL SALAD WITH PORK & PICKLED CARROTS

CRISPY BASIL SALAD WITH PORK & PICKLED CARROTS

A fusion of Thai and Chinese, this salad is packed with great zingy flavours. To save time, make the pickled carrots in advance and refrigerate until needed.

Serves 2

- 500ml groundnut oil
- 300g minced pork
- A pinch of ground white pepper
- 3 spring onions, finely sliced, reserving one to serve
- 1 tbsp red thai paste
- 300ml chicken stock
- A small cube of bread, to test the oil
- 1 bunch holy basil, leaves picked (see note)
- 1 head gem or iceberg lettuce, leaves separated

Pickled carrots

- 200ml rice vinegar
- 100g sugar
- 1 tsp fennel seeds
- 1 star anise
- 2 medium carrots, finely sliced with a mandolin

1 To make the pickled carrots, add the rice vinegar to a saucepan over a medium heat with the sugar, fennel seeds, star anise, and 1 teaspoon of sea salt. Bring to a simmer and stir until the sugar has dissolved. Remove from the heat, tip in the carrots and stir to coat. Leave to cool completely, then set aside to pickle for at least 30 minutes.
2 Heat 1 tablespoon of the groundnut oil in a wok until smoking hot. Add the minced pork, season with the white pepper and a pinch of salt, then toss until golden and starting to crisp.
3 Add 2 of the chopped spring onions and the red thai paste, and cook for 1 minute. Pour in the stock and turn down the heat, cooking for a further 20 minutes, or until the stock has

SPANISH-STYLE AUBERGINE, PEPPER & JAMON SALAD WITH PAPRIKA DRESSING

Serves 4

- 2 slices of jamon serrano, roughly torn
- 40g hard goat's cheese, thinly sliced
- 1 x 150g jar of red piquillo peppers, drained and cut into strips
- 1 x 150g jar of grilled aubergines, drained and cut into strips
- 2 handfuls of castelfranco or other large salad leaves
- ½ bunch of watercress

Paprika dressing

- 2 tbsp sherry vinegar
- 4 tbsp extra virgin olive oil
- ¼ tsp ground cumin
- ¼ tsp paprika

1 Whisk together all of the dressing ingredients in a bowl with some sea salt.
2 Put the jamon serrano, goat's cheese, piquillo peppers, aubergine, salad leaves and watercress in a serving bowl. Add the paprika dressing, toss together and serve immediately.

Per serving 194 cals, 17.3g fat (4g saturated), 4.5g protein, 4.2g carbs, 3.6g sugars

SPANISH-STYLE AUBERGINE, PEPPER &
JAMON SALAD WITH PAPRIKA DRESSING

ASIAN SEAFOOD SALAD WITH YUZU & SESAME DRESSING

WARM PARSNIP & POTATO
SALAD WITH VIGNOTTE

BRAISED SPRING VEG

ASIAN SEAFOOD SALAD WITH YUZU & SESAME DRESSING

You can find yuzu (a Japanese citrus fruit) juice in good supermarkets and Asian stores, otherwise use lime juice.

Serves 4

- ½ tbsp olive oil
- 1 squid, cleaned and sliced
- ½ tbsp soy sauce
- 250g cooked octopus, sliced
- 8 prawns, cooked and peeled
- A generous handful of salad leaves
- A small handful of edible flowers

Yuzu & sesame dressing

- 3 tbsp toasted sesame oil
- ½ tbsp soy sauce
- 1 tbsp yuzu juice, or juice of ½ lime
- 1 tsp togarashi spice mix
- 1 tbsp sesame seeds, toasted

1 Heat the oil in a small frying pan over a medium heat, add the squid and cook for 3-4 minutes. Turn the heat up to high, add the soy and stir continuously for 2 minutes, or until the squid is tender and coated in soy. Transfer to a bowl.
2 Combine all of the dressing ingredients in another bowl. Put the squid, octopus, prawns and salad leaves in a salad bowl. Add the dressing and mix well. Sprinkle with the edible flowers and serve.

Per serving 213 cals, 14.2g fat (2.2g saturated), 19.7g protein, 14.3g carbs, 0.6g sugars

BRAISED SPRING VEG

Serves 6 as a side

- 100g coarse breadcrumbs
- Extra virgin olive oil
- 4 garlic cloves, finely sliced
- A small bunch of parsley, leaves picked and chopped, stalks finely chopped
- 200g baby leeks, cut in half lengthways
- 2 x 200g packs of baby courgettes, sliced into 1cm-thick discs
- 1 large glass of white wine
- 1 x 230g bunch of asparagus, stalks trimmed and sliced, tips intact
- 150g fresh peas
- 150g fresh broad beans
- Juice and zest of 1 lemon
- Fat-free yoghurt, to serve

1 Toast the breadcrumbs in a dry frying pan until golden. Set aside in a bowl.
2 Heat a glug of oil in a large, lidded, non-stick frying pan over a medium heat. Add the garlic, parsley stalks and leeks, and sauté for 10 minutes until the leeks are soft and translucent.
3 Add the courgettes, then the wine, and bring to the boil. Reduce the heat, cover and simmer for 5 minutes.
4 Add the asparagus, peas and broad beans to the pan, season well and sweat for 7-8 minutes over a low heat.
5 Grate the lemon zest into the toasted breadcrumbs and add the parsley leaves.

Squeeze the lemon juice over the veg and serve topped with the breadcrumb mixture and a dollop of yoghurt.

Per serving 192 cals, 4.7g fat (0.7g saturated), 8.4g protein, 19.8g carbs, 4.3g sugars

WARM PARSNIP & POTATO SALAD WITH VIGNOTTE

Vignotte is a rich, tangy French cheese. If you can't find it, you could use a mild goat's cheese instead.

Serves 2

- 4 parsnips, quartered and cored
- 300g new potatoes, quartered
- 4 tbsp olive oil
- 200g smoked streaky bacon
- 2 tbsp baby capers, drained and rinsed
- A handful of herbs (such as dill or chives), chopped
- 1 tbsp balsamic vinegar
- 150g vignotte, chopped

1 Preheat the oven to 180C/gas 4. Coat the vegetables in half the oil and season. Roast for 20-30 minutes until tender.
2 Grill the bacon, then mix together in a bowl with the roast vegetables, capers, herbs, balsamic vinegar and remaining oil. Top with the cheese and any leftover dressing. Serve with crusty bread.

Per serving 1062 cals, 72.2g fat (26g saturated), 40g protein, 65.4g carbs, 22.6g sugars

LENTIL & VEGGIE STEW

- 50g mixed seeds
- Olive oil
- ½ tsp sweet smoked paprika
- 2 knobs of unsalted butter
- Zest and juice of 1 orange
- ¼ tsp ground cinnamon
- 150g golden caster sugar
- 2 handfuls of salad leaves

Buttermilk dressing
- 75ml buttermilk
- Juice of 1 lemon
- ½ bunch of mixed soft herbs, such
  as chervil, tarragon and mint, leaves
  picked and chopped

1 Give your beetroots a good clean, then place in a large pan and cover with cold water. Bring to the boil over a high heat, then cover, reduce to a simmer and cook for about 1 hour, until soft. Drain and set aside to cool. As soon as they are cool enough to handle, peel off the skins and cut roughly into 3cm wedges.
2 While the beetroots are cooking, toss the seeds in a little olive oil, the paprika and a pinch of sea salt and black pepper; toast in a dry frying pan until golden. Remove from the pan and set aside.
3 Make the dressing by whisking the buttermilk in a jug with the juice of half the lemon and a good glug of olive oil. Season, stir in the herbs and set aside.
4 Melt the butter in the frying pan you toasted the seeds in and add the orange zest. Add a squeeze of orange juice, the cinnamon and sugar and a good pinch of salt and pepper. Bring to the boil and bubble for around 10 minutes until sticky and caramelised. Remove from the heat and toss through the cooked beets. Leave to cool slightly, then transfer to a platter.
5 Toss the salad leaves with the dressing and scatter over the beets. Finish with the toasted seeds.

Per serving 465 cals, 21.4g fat (6.9g saturated), 8.1g protein, 56.1g carbs, 52.7g sugars

LENTIL & VEGGIE STEW

Serves 4
- 1 tbsp olive oil
- 1 onion, sliced
- ½ tsp chilli flakes
- 1 bouquet garni
- 3 garlic cloves, crushed
- 250g puy lentils, rinsed
- 800ml hot stock
- 200g Tenderstem broccoli,
  roughly chopped
- 150g green beans, trimmed
  and halved
- 2 large carrots, cut into batons
- A handful of cherry tomatoes
- 2 handfuls of spinach or winter
  greens, chopped
- 2 tbsp red wine vinegar
- Extra-virgin olive oil
- Pecorino and bread, to serve (optional)

1 Heat the oil in a casserole and add the onion, chilli and bouquet garni. Cook over a medium heat, stirring often, until the onion is softened.
2 Add garlic and cook for a further 1-2 minutes then add the lentils and stock. Bring to the boil then reduce to a simmer for 15 minutes. Add the broccoli, beans, carrots and tomatoes and cook for a further 8-10 minutes or until the lentils and veg are cooked but have some bite.
3 Remove from the heat and stir in the spinach until wilted. Stir through the vinegar and season. Serve in bowls with a drizzle of extra virgin olive oil, a grating of pecorino, and fresh bread, if you like.

Per serving 325 cals, 7.5g fat (1.1g saturated), 21g protein, 45.6g carbs, 9.3g sugars

CANDIED BEET SALAD WITH BUTTERMILK DRESSING

Serves 4
- 750g golden or candy cane beetroot
  (or a mix of both)

CANDIED BEET SALAD WITH BUTTERMILK DRESSING

GRIDDLED VEGETABLES & FETA WITH TABBOULEH

Serves 8

- 150g feta cheese
- ½ bunch of oregano, leaves picked
- Olive oil
- 2 red onions, sliced into wedges
- 1 large aubergine, halved lengthways
- 3 courgettes (yellow and green)
- 2 handfuls of tomatoes (a mixture of sizes and colours)
- 1 garlic bulb
- 1 small bunch of flat leaf parsley, leaves picked
- 50g shelled whole pistachio nuts
- 2 tbsp runny honey
- Flatbreads, to serve (optional)

Tabbouleh
- 250g cracked wheat
- 1 bunch of mint, leaves picked and finely chopped
- 1 large bunch of flat leaf parsley, leaves picked and finely chopped
- ½ cucumber, finely chopped
- 1 lemon
- Extra virgin olive oil

1 Light your barbecue and give the coals time to get nice and hot. Add the feta to a bowl with half the oregano leaves, a drizzle of oil and a good pinch of sea salt and black pepper. Set aside to marinate.
2 Meanwhile make the tabbouleh. Cook the cracked wheat according to packet instructions, then rinse and drain. Set aside to cool a little.
3 Mix in the mint, parsley and cucumber, a squeeze of lemon juice and a pinch of salt and pepper. Cover and set aside.
4 When your barbecue is hot enough to start cooking, grill all of the veg and garlic and, once beautifully charred on both sides, transfer them to a chopping board. Chop all the veg together, squeeze the garlic cloves out of their skins and squish the tomatoes. Roughly chop the parsley and remaining oregano into the vegetables, season and drizzle with oil.
5 Carefully griddle the whole marinated feta on the barbecue for about 3 minutes (this will depend how hot your barbecue is), or until golden and crispy, then gently turn and cook for another 1-2 minutes.
6 Toast the pistachios in a small pan over a medium heat until lightly golden, then spoon over the honey and allow the nuts

MOROCCAN CUCUMBER, CARROT & CHICKPEA SALAD

to caramelise, tossing regularly to stop them from catching. (Don't be tempted to touch them - they will be very hot!) After a couple of minutes, tip them onto a sheet of oiled greaseproof paper to harden, then roughly chop and set aside.
7 Spoon the tabbouleh onto a large serving dish and top with the chopped veg. Place the griddled feta in the centre, drizzle with a little extra virgin olive oil and scatter over the crispy smashed pistachios. Crumble the feta over the top and serve with toasted flatbreads.
Per serving 215 cals, 9.8g fat (3.4g saturated), 8.9g protein, 20.6g carbs, 10.5g sugars

----

MOROCCAN CUCUMBER, CARROT & CHICKPEA SALAD

Serves 2

- 1 cucumber, halved lengthways
- 2 small carrots
- 1 x 400g tin of chickpeas, drained and rinsed
- 25g dried cherries, roughly chopped
- 1 large bunch of mint, leaves picked
- 1 large bunch of dill, leaves picked

Dressing
- 1 tsp coriander seeds
- 1 tsp honey
- Juice of ½ lemon
- 3 tbsp extra virgin olive oil
- 50g blanched hazelnuts

1 Scrape out and discard the middle of the cucumber; finely slice into half moons, then place in a bowl. Very thinly slice the carrots (try a mandoline) and add to the bowl with the chickpeas, cherries, mint and dill, and mix well.
2 Gently toast the coriander seeds in a dry pan, then pound with a pestle and mortar. Shake in a jam jar with the honey, lemon juice, olive oil and salt and pepper.
3 Toast the hazelnuts until golden, then roughly chop. Toss the dressing and salad in a serving bowl and add the nuts.
Per serving 676 cals, 41.1g fat (4.8g saturated), 20.7g protein, 57.1g carbs, 24.9g sugars

FAVA BEAN PUREE WITH
BAKED GREENS & CHILLI

NICOISE SALAD
WITH CONFIT TUNA
& CAPER DRESSING

FAVA BEAN PUREE WITH BAKED GREENS & CHILLI

Serves 4-6 as a side or 8 as a starter

- 500g dried split fava beans, or 800g frozen broad beans, or 2 x 400g tins of foul medames (see note)
- 1 onion, halved
- 2 tbsp semolina flour

Wild greens

- 4 garlic cloves, finely sliced
- 500g wild greens, chard or cavolo nero, stalks chopped, leaves left whole
- A handful of grated pecorino

Chilli oil

- 3 dried red chillies
- 250ml extra virgin olive oil

1 Rinse the fava beans. If using frozen broad beans, blanch for 30 seconds and, when cool, remove the skins.
2 Put the beans in a pan with the onion and season well. Just cover with water and heat gently for 30 minutes, stirring in the semolina flour halfway through.
3 Preheat the oven to 180C/gas 4 and heat a glug of oil in a large ovenproof pan over a medium heat. Add the garlic and fry for 1-2 minutes, until lightly golden. Stir in the chopped stalks and fry for 5 minutes, until softened but not coloured, then add the leaves and 750ml of water. Season, bring to the boil and simmer for 10 minutes, until softened but slightly al

dente. If the greens are watery, strain off the excess liquid. Stir well and sprinkle over the pecorino. Bake for 15 minutes.
4 At the same time make the chilli oil. Blitz the dried chillies with a little of the olive oil in a blender to make a paste, add the remaining oil, blitz again and store in a sterilised bottle or jar until needed.
5 When the beans are cooked, transfer to a food processor with a splash of the cooking water, discarding the onion. Blitz to a purée, adding a splash of water until it's a creamy consistency. Serve with the wild greens and a drizzle of chilli oil.
Note If you are making this with tinned fava beans (foul medames), just drain them, remove the skins, then follow the rest of the method above.
Per serving 288 cals, 9.2g fat (2.4g saturated), 17.7g protein, 27.9g carbs, 5.7g sugars

NICOISE SALAD WITH CONFIT TUNA & CAPER DRESSING

Serves 6

- 1 small head of fennel, including fronds, thinly sliced
- 350g small potatoes, scrubbed, boiled and halved
- 350g green beans, trimmed and boiled
- 2 tbsp small olives
- 12 cherry tomatoes, halved
- 12 quail eggs, boiled, peeled and halved

- 2 large handfuls of frisée or other salad leaves, washed and dried

Confit tuna

- 500g fresh tuna
- 2 garlic cloves, unpeeled
- 3 sprigs of fresh thyme
- Zest of 1 lemon
- Extra virgin olive oil (about 500ml)

Caper dressing

- 6 tbsp extra virgin olive oil
- 1½ tbsp capers, drained
- Juice of 1 lemon
- ½ tbsp white wine vinegar

1 To make the confit tuna, put the tuna in a bowl, sprinkle with 1 tablespoon of sea salt and cover with cold water. Chill overnight or for at least 6 hours.
2 Drain the tuna, transfer to a snug-fitting pan, add the garlic, thyme and lemon zest, and cover with olive oil. Cook over a medium heat for about 5 minutes, until the oil is bubbling. Turn the heat to low, simmer for 10 minutes, then turn off the heat and allow to cool. Transfer the tuna and oil to a Kilner jar and chill.
3 Put the fennel, potatoes, beans, olives, tomatoes, eggs and frisée in a salad bowl.
4 Mix all of the dressing ingredients in a small bowl and season well.
5 Flake the confit tuna into the salad, season and gently toss in the dressing.
Per serving 377 cals, 23.1g fat (4.4g saturated), 27.5g protein, 12.4g carbs, 3g sugars

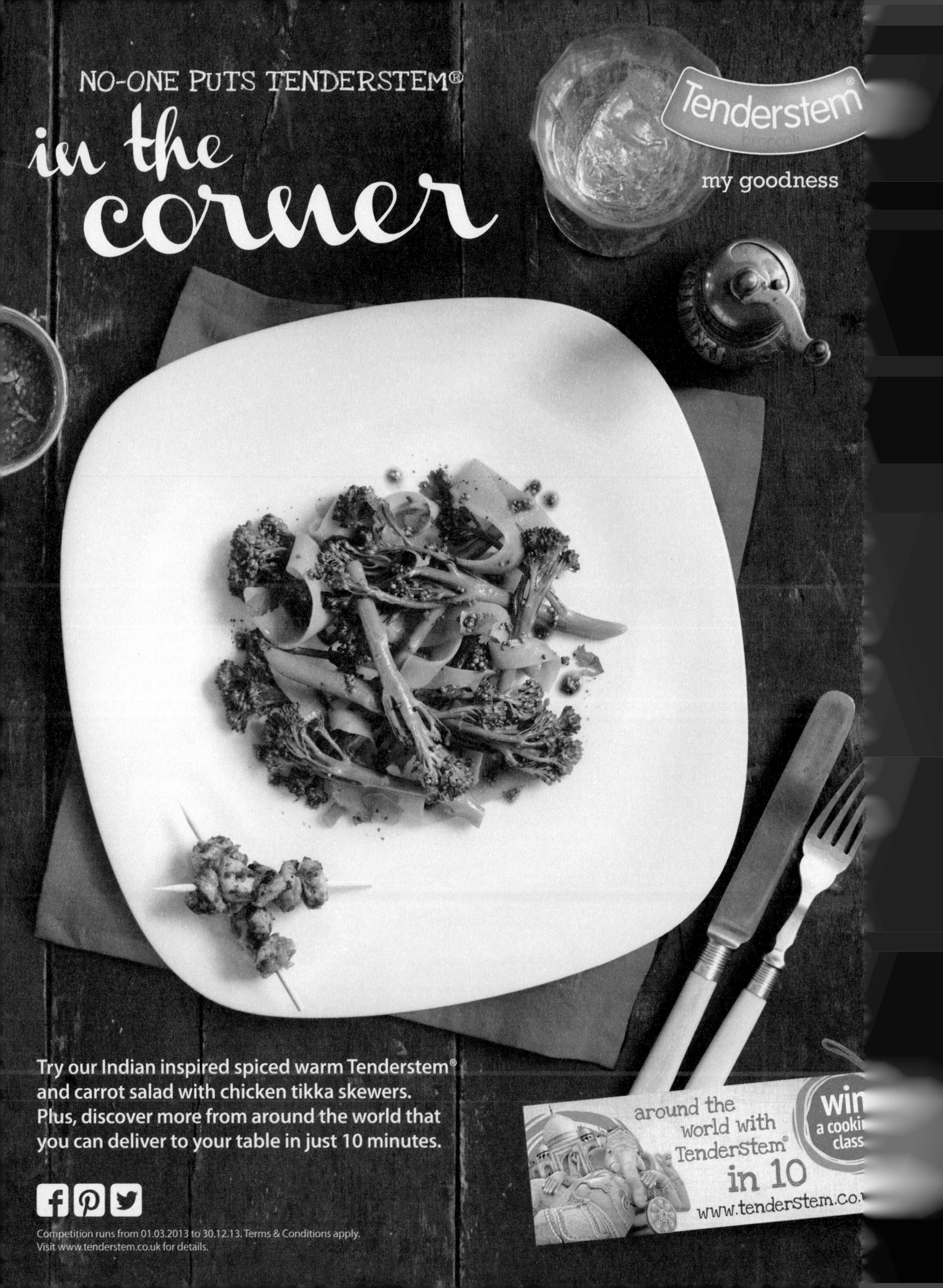

NO-ONE PUTS TENDERSTEM®
in the corner
Tenderstem®
my goodness
Try our Indian inspired spiced warm Tenderstem® and carrot salad with chicken tikka skewers. Plus, discover more from around the world that you can deliver to your table in just 10 minutes.
around the world with Tenderstem® in 10
www.tenderstem.co.
win a cooki class
Competition runs from 01.03.2013 to 30.12.13. Terms & Conditions apply. Visit www.tenderstem.co.uk for details.

AUBERGINE & HALLOUMI BURGERS
WITH HARISSA YOGHURT

BAKED BEANS

GOAT'S CURD, FIG & WALNUT SALAD

AUBERGINE & HALLOUMI BURGERS WITH HARISSA YOGHURT

Serves 4

- 5 baby aubergines or one large aubergine
- 1 tsp cumin seeds
- 2 tbsp olive oil
- 4 sprigs of thyme, leaves only
- 1 tbsp sumac
- 1 garlic clove, sliced
- 1 x 250g pack of halloumi
- 1 tbsp harissa
- 100ml yoghurt
- 4 ciabatta rolls, halved
- 1 little gem lettuce, sliced

1 Slice the aubergines (lengthways if baby; into discs if large) and put in a bowl with the cumin, oil, thyme, sumac and garlic. Season, toss to coat and set aside to rest for at least 30 minutes.
2 Slice the halloumi into about 12 pieces. In a bowl, mix the harissa with the yoghurt. Heat a griddle pan and cook the aubergine slices for 3-4 minutes on each side, until tender and charred. Cook halloumi for 2-3 minutes on each side.
3 Briefly griddle the rolls, then fill with the halloumi, aubergines, harissa yoghurt and lettuce.

Per serving 517 cals, 27.2g fat (12.9g saturated), 25.3g protein, 47g carbs, 7.2g sugars

BAKED BEANS

Serves 6

- 250g dried cannellini or haricot beans (or 1 x 400g tin of cannellini beans)
- 2 tbsp olive oil (1 tbsp if using the pancetta)
- 1 red onion, finely chopped
- 2 garlic cloves, finely chopped
- 75g pancetta, finely chopped (optional)
- 1 bay leaf
- 1 tbsp tomato purée
- A pinch of smoked paprika
- 2 tbsp red wine vinegar
- 1 x 400g tin chopped tomatoes
- 1 tbsp soft dark brown sugar
- Toasted slices of sourdough bread and grated parmesan, to serve

1 If using dried beans, soak overnight in plenty of cold water. Drain and add to a large, heavy pan with enough cold water to cover by 2-3cm. Bring to the boil, skim off any foam, then reduce the heat and simmer for 30-40 minutes, or until tender. Drain and set aside.
2 To a large pan, add the oil, onion, garlic, pancetta (if using) and bay leaf. Cook over a medium heat for 5-8 minutes, or until the onion is softened and the pancetta is getting crisp. Add the tomato purée and paprika, and cook for 1 minute, then add the vinegar, tomatoes and sugar. Season and bring to the boil, add the beans (or drained tinned beans, if using) and cook for 20-25 minutes, or until the beans are tender and the sauce is thick. Serve on toasted sourdough with a sprinkling of parmesan.

Per serving 370 cals, 27g fat (3.9g saturated), 7.2g protein, 23.2g carbs, 12.1g sugars

GOAT'S CURD, FIG & WALNUT SALAD

Serves 2

- 2 litres goat's milk
- Juice of 1 lemon
- 2 handfuls of chicory or radicchio
- 100g walnut halves, toasted
- 2 ripe figs, cut into quarters
- Extra virgin olive oil
- Balsamic vinegar

1 Bring the goat's milk to a simmer in a large pan. The moment it starts to boil, add the lemon juice. Cook for a minute or 2 to allow the milk to curdle, then remove from the heat. Strain through a sieve lined with a muslin cloth or clean J-cloth. Allow all of the liquid (whey) to drain off and squeeze out any excess.
2 Combine the salad leaves, walnuts and figs. Divide between plates, top with the goat's curd, and drizzle over some extra virgin olive oil and balsamic vinegar.

Per serving 712 cals, 56g fat (16.2g saturated), 23.6g protein, 29.7g carbs, 28.7g sugars

"The beauty of the Dome60 is that it's smaller and more affordable than most wood ovens out there, but still beautifully made and large enough to do all the jobs you'd expect from a wood-fired oven – you name it."

Jamie O

WOOD FIRED OVENS
— BY JAMIE OLIVER —

For al fresco dining with a difference, upgrade your barbecue and invest in a compact wood-fired oven. Exclusive to Jamie Oliver, the Dome60 outdoor oven is manufactured by a company based in southern Italy. Delivered in a beautiful box made from sustainable wood, the Dome60 comes with an easy-to-assemble stand and all the equipment you need to get started. In fact, its fuss-free design means you can be cooking your first meal in it within a matter of hours. At £1,200 the Dome60 is a great investment piece for any garden or terrace – the price includes VAT, kerb-side delivery (UK only), as well as a pizza paddle, brush, fire-starter kit (UK only) and instructional handbook with great recipes to get you inspired. Plus, each oven comes with an individual serial number and a Made in Italy certification, so you know you're cooking with quality. **To find out more about the Dome60, or to buy, go online to jamieoliverovens.com or call 020 3375 5399 in the UK**

FISH & SEAFOOD

Whether you're serious about salmon, prefer prawns, or have a craving for crab, you'll love these seafood dishes. Keep it simple with pan-fried red mullet, or indulge in our lobster rolls – there's a veritable ocean of choice

THAI CUTTLEFISH
STIR-FRY WITH PAK CHOI

SEARED TUNA, LENTIL &
SUN-DRIED TOMATO SALAD

THAI CUTTLEFISH STIR-FRY WITH PAK CHOI

Serves 4

- 1 medium cuttlefish
- A thumb-sized piece of ginger, peeled
- 1 garlic clove
- 1 stick of lemongrass
- 1 red chilli
- 4 spring onions
- 1 tbsp sesame oil
- 1 tsp fish sauce
- 4 pak choi
- 2 limes
- Thai basil, to serve

1 Place the cuttlefish on a board. Pull the head hard away from the body, which will pull out some of the internal organs. Discard these. Cut through the base of the head to remove the eyes; discard these but keep the tentacles.
2 Pull out anything left inside. Remove the hard flat bone and discard this, too. Wash the cuttlefish under the tap and return to the cleaned chopping board.
3 Remove and discard the outer membrane (peel it off with your fingers). Slice the flesh into strips and set aside.
4 Chop the ginger and garlic, then the lemongrass, red chilli and spring onions. Heat the oil in a wok over a medium heat, add the chopped ingredients and stir-fry for 1 minute. Add the fish sauce and

cuttlefish and stir-fry for 3 minutes. Drop in the pak choi and let it wilt. Squeeze over the juice of 1 lime, then serve with lime wedges and Thai basil.

Per serving 160 cals, 4g fat (0g saturated), 25g protein, 1g carbs, 1g sugars

SEARED TUNA, LENTIL & SUN-DRIED TOMATO SALAD

Serves 2

- 2 tuna steaks
- 3 tbsp extra virgin olive oil
- 250g ready-to-eat puy lentils
- A handful each of chopped basil leaves and parsley
- 1 avocado, sliced
- 1½ tbsp small capers
- 100g sun-dried tomatoes in oil, chopped
- Balsamic vinegar

1 Season the tuna lightly with salt, pepper and 1 tablespoon of oil. Sear the tuna in a dry pan over a high heat for 1½ minutes each side for pink, or 3 minutes for cooked through. Set aside to rest.
2 Microwave the lentils for 2½ minutes. Break the tuna into chunks. Arrange on plates with the lentils, herbs, avocado, capers and tomatoes. Drizzle with the rest of the oil and some balsamic vinegar.

Per serving 969 cals, 41g fat (17.7g saturated), 52.4g protein, 91g carbs, 26.6g sugars

SALMON WITH SMOKY PEPPER SAUCE & POTATO SALAD

Serves 4

- 2 roasted peppers from a jar, drained
- 1 garlic clove
- ½ tsp smoked paprika
- A pinch of chilli flakes
- 100ml extra virgin olive oil
- 3–4 tbsp sherry vinegar
- 500g new potatoes
- 400g fine green beans
- 1 shallot, finely chopped
- A handful of pitted olives, halved
- 1–2 lemons
- 4 salmon steaks, skin on

1 In a food processor whizz up the peppers, garlic, paprika and chilli. Stir in enough oil to loosen, season with salt and pepper, and add vinegar to taste.
2 Cook the potatoes in salted water for 15 minutes or until tender, throw in the beans and cook for 2–3 minutes. Drain, tip into a bowl and add the shallot, olives, a glug of olive oil and a squeeze of lemon.
3 Meanwhile, season and lightly oil the salmon, squeeze over some lemon and grill on a foil-lined grill pan, skin side up, for 5-6 minutes. The skin should be crisp and the flesh just cooked through. Serve with the salad and drizzle over the sauce.

Per serving 726 cals, 48.7g fat (7.7g saturated), 40.4g protein, 33g carbs, 1.6g sugars

SALMON WITH SMOKY PEPPER
SAUCE & POTATO SALAD

MIXED FISH GRILL &
DECONSTRUCTED PAELLA

MIXED FISH GRILL & DECONSTRUCTED PAELLA

A great one for the summer barbecue.

Serves 4-6

- Olive oil
- 2 whole gurnard, gutted, cleaned and trimmed (ask your fishmonger to do this)
- 2 lemons, sliced
- A handful of fresh herbs, such as thyme, flat leaf parsley, basil and marjoram
- 4 baby squid, tentacles on, cleaned (ask your fishmonger to do this)
- A handful of clams
- 12 mussels
- 4 oysters
- A handful of fresh peas in their pods, to serve
- Lemon wedges, to serve

Saffron rice
- 500g paella rice
- A pinch of saffron

Pepper & chilli salsa
- 2 peppers (red and orange)
- 2 red chillies, pricked
- 4 spring onions
- 1 small bunch of flat leaf parsley
- A splash of red wine vinegar
- Extra virgin olive oil

1 Light your barbecue and get yourself a nice bed of glowing hot coals (you may want to put a large wire cooling rack onto your barbecue, if the bars are far apart, as you are going to cook and serve everything straight on the rack). Brush the bars of your barbecue or rack with oil to stop the fish from sticking.
2 Make the salsa by cooking the peppers and chillies on the barbecue until the skins are blackened, then transfer to a bowl and cover with cling film. Once cool enough to handle, peel away the skin (don't be tempted to wash the skin off, as this will take away a lot of the flavour). Chop the peppers and chillies with the spring onions and parsley, then dress with the vinegar, 3 tablespoons of olive oil and a pinch of seasoning.
3 Season the gurnards inside and out with sea salt and black pepper, drizzle with olive oil, then fill the cavities with lemon slices and the herbs.
4 Cut open the squid and open it out like a book, then lightly score the

underside in a criss-cross pattern using a blunt knife.
5 Cook the paella rice according to the packet instructions, adding a pinch of saffron while cooking.
6 Place the gurnard on the bars of the barbecue (or cooling rack, if using), then, after a couple of minutes, add all the other seafood. The gurnards will take about 3-5 minutes each side - be gentle when flipping them over. Cook the squid for about 1 minute each side, until opaque. Cook the shellfish until the shells open up, about 5-7 minutes.
7 Once all the fish is ready and the clams and mussels have opened (discard any that haven't), serve the grill on a tray in the centre of the table scattered with some freshly chopped flat leaf parsley. Serve with the saffron rice, pepper and chilli salsa, fresh peas and lots of lemon wedges for squeezing over.

Per serving 761 cals, 9.7g fat (2.5g saturated), 46.6g protein, 107.3g carbs, 7.3g sugars

GRAPEFRUIT, CRAB & BEETROOT SALAD

GRAPEFRUIT, CRAB & BEETROOT SALAD

Serves 4

- 1kg crab, boiled
- 1 handful of frisée lettuce
- 1 handful of rocket
- 200g beetroot, boiled, peeled and thinly sliced
- 1 grapefruit, segmented
- 1 pink grapefruit, segmented
- 4 tbsp extra virgin olive oil

1 Carefully remove the meat from the cooked crab, cracking the claws, too, making sure no shell gets into the meat. Pop it in a bowl and set aside.
2 To assemble the salad, arrange the frisée, rocket, beetroot, white and pink grapefruit segments and crab meat on a platter, drizzle over the olive oil, season with freshly ground black pepper, and serve.

Per serving 498 cals, 25.9g fat (3.5g saturated), 51.2g protein, 13.2g carbs, 12.7g sugars

- 1kg mussels, cleaned
- 4 ripe vine tomatoes
- 500g maris piper potatoes, peeled
- Finely grated zest of 1 lemon
- 2 onions, peeled and finely sliced
- Pecorino, for grating
- 300g risotto rice
- 1½-2 litres vegetable stock

1 Preheat the oven to 180C/gas 4. In a large saucepan, heat a glug of olive oil over a medium heat, then sauté 1 garlic clove and all of the parsley stalks for 2 minutes, or until lightly golden. Add the mussels, cover with a lid, and leave them to open (about 3 minutes).
2 Take the pan off the heat, then strain the mussels through a sieve, saving the juice for later and discarding unopened mussels. Remove the empty half shell from each mussel, so they are half exposed. Set aside.
3 Skin the tomatoes by placing them in a bowl and covering with boiling water. Leave until you can see the skin starting to come away. Drain, then plunge into cold water. Once they are cool enough, peel and roughly chop. Set aside.
4 Thinly slice the potatoes, then toss with a drizzle of olive oil, the lemon zest, and a little black pepper. In a separate bowl, mix together the chopped parsley leaves and the remaining garlic.
5 Take a large ovenproof dish, drizzle a little oil in the bottom and scatter in the onion and half the chopped tomatoes. Sprinkle over half the parsley mix, then layer half of the sliced potatoes, and finely grate over a little pecorino.
6 Arrange the mussels on top, so they're pointing upwards, and scatter over the rice. Season - not too much salt, they're quite salty already - then sprinkle with the remaining parsley mix and tomatoes.
7 Layer on the rest of the potatoes, then pour over the mussel juice and top with enough vegetable stock to reach the potatoes. Finish by finely grating over a layer of pecorino, drizzle with olive oil and cover tightly with foil.
8 Bake in the oven for 35-40 minutes. until the rice and potatoes are cooked through, then remove the foil and bake for a further 10 minutes, until golden. Serve immediately.

Per serving 433 cals, 6.4 g fat (1.4g saturated), 28.8g protein, 63.1g carbs, 5.7g sugars

SMOKED SALMON FISHCAKES WITH DILL & LEMON DRESSING

SMOKED SALMON FISHCAKES WITH DILL & LEMON DRESSING

Makes 8

- 3 maris piper potatoes, peeled and cut into 5cm chunks
- 20g dill, finely chopped
- 4 spring onions, finely chopped
- 200g smoked salmon, chopped
- 1 tbsp mini capers
- 1 egg, beaten
- 2 tbsp rice flour
- 150g panko breadcrumbs
- Vegetable oil for shallow frying

Dill & lemon dressing

- 20g dill
- 1 garlic clove
- 150ml sour cream
- Juice of 1 lemon, zest of ½

1 Boil, drain then mash the potatoes. Mix in the spring onions, salmon, capers and dill. Chill in the fridge for 20 minutes.
2 Place the beaten egg in a shallow bowl, the flour in a second, and the breadcrumbs in a third. Using your hands, form the potato mixture into patties and carefully coat each one in the flour, then the egg, then the crumbs.
3 Fill a shallow non-stick pan with vegetable oil to about 2cm and place over a medium heat. Once hot, fry each fishcake for about 2-3 minutes on each side, until golden. Drain on kitchen towel.
4 For the dressing, blitz the dill, garlic, sour cream, lemon juice and zest, and serve with the fishcakes.

Per serving 234 cals, 9.5g fat (3.2g saturated), 11.7g protein, 28.2g carbs, 1.5g sugars

TIELLA

Serves 6

- Extra virgin olive oil
- 2 garlic cloves, peeled and finely chopped
- A large bunch of parsley, leaves picked and stalks finely chopped

TIELLA

CAUSA CROQUETTES

CAUSA CROQUETTES

Makes 15

- 750g potatoes, peeled
- A large knob of unsalted butter
- 1 red onion, finely chopped
- Juice and zest of 1 lime
- 200g small cooked prawns
- 100g white crabmeat
- 1–2 tsp aji amarillo paste (see note) or piri piri sauce
- 100g flour
- 2 eggs, beaten
- 100g breadcrumbs
- 1 litre vegetable oil
- A cube of bread, to test the oil

Avocado dressing

- 2 ripe avocadoes
- 2 limes
- 1 red onion
- 1 ripe tomato
- 1 bunch of coriander
- Extra virgin olive oil

1 Cut the potatoes into even-sized chunks, then place in a large pan of cold salted water. Bring to the boil, then cook over a medium heat for 15–20 minutes, until tender. Drain and steam dry, then mash the potatoes until really smooth (use a potato ricer if you have one). Season well and mash in the butter.
2 Now make the guacamole-style dressing. Scrape the avocado flesh into a medium-sized bowl, discarding the stones and skins, season with salt and pepper and squeeze over the juice of the 2 limes. Grate in the onion and tomato, then mash together to a chunky guacamole. Chop the coriander and add it to the guacamole with plenty of extra virgin olive oil, then leave to one side.
3 Place the finely chopped red onion in a small bowl, add the juice and zest of 1 lime, toss together and leave to one side for 5–10 minutes. Finely chop the prawns and mix together with the crabmeat and aji amarillo paste, seasoning well. Mix the onions into the bowl with the prawns, leaving behind the excess juice.
4 Line up 3 bowls - one with the flour, one with the beaten eggs and one with the breadcrumbs. Place a scoop of mashed potato in your hand and roll into a ball (roughly 4cm in diameter). Press a hole in the middle with your thumb about 2cm deep and spoon in some of

RED MULLET, SPINACH & LEMON

the prawn and crab mixture. Close the hole as gently as you can to conceal the filling, then repeat until you've used up all the mash and filling - you should end up with around 15 croquettes.
5 Roll each croquette in the flour, then dip into the egg (letting the excess drip off), then coat in breadcrumbs.
6 Pour the vegetable oil into a large pan and gently heat to 180C, or until a cube of bread dropped into the oil turns brown within 1 minute. Gently lower the croquettes into the oil with a slotted spoon and fry for around 7 minutes, or until golden and crisp - you'll need to do this in batches. Drain the cooked croquettes on some kitchen paper, then serve hot on a plate smeared with the guacamole.

Note Aji amarillo paste is made from mild orange chillies. Find it in specialist stores or buy online at mexgrocer.co.uk.

Per serving 261 cals, 17.1g fat (3g saturated), 7.7g protein, 18g carbs, 2.3g sugars

RED MULLET, SPINACH & LEMON

Serves 2

- Olive oil
- 1 lemon, sliced very thinly
- Juice of ½ lemon
- 4 red mullet fillets
- 1 large bag of spinach

1 Pour 2 tablespoons of olive oil into a large frying pan and place over a medium heat. Add the lemon slices and sprinkle them with a pinch of sea salt.
2 Turn the lemons once then add the juice to the pan. Once caramelised, remove and add the fish. Cook for 3 minutes each side, until cooked through and the skin is crisp. Transfer to a plate.
3 Wilt the spinach in the same pan, then place in a serving bowl. Place the fish on top and strew the lemons and their sauce over everything.

Per serving 387 cals, 21.7g fat (2g saturated), 41.5g protein, 3.6g carbs, 3.6g sugars

ACORDA DE MARISCOS

GRILLED LOBSTER ROLLS

ACORDA DE MARISCOS
Serves 6-8
- 3 thick doorsteps of stale bread, roughly torn (about 250g)
- 150ml red wine vinegar
- 150ml olive oil
- 2 tsp ground cumin
- 350g shelled king prawns, cooked
- 1 cucumber, peeled and roughly chopped
- 1 medium red onion, chopped small
- 3 medium tomatoes, diced
- About 20 green olives
- 5 garlic cloves, chopped small
- 3 tbsp chopped coriander

1 Place the bread in a large bowl. In a jug, combine the vinegar, olive oil and cumin with 200ml of water. Drizzle this mixture over the bread and leave for 5 minutes for the flavours to get to know each other and the bread to soften.
2 Once the bread is moist and the flavours absorbed, add the rest of the ingredients and toss to combine.
Per serving 424 cals, 5.4g sugars, 27.7g fat (4.2g saturated), 16.2g protein, 24.6g carbs

GRILLED LOBSTER ROLLS
Serves 6
- 85g butter, softened
- 6 hot dog buns
- 500g cooked lobster meat, chopped
- 50g celery, diced
- 2 tbsp mayonnaise
- ½ iceberg lettuce, shredded

1 Preheat a griddle pan until really hot. Butter the hot dog buns on both sides and grill on both sides until toasted and lightly charred (keep an eye on them so they don't burn).
2 In a bowl, mix together the lobster meat, celery and mayonnaise, and season with sea salt and freshly ground black pepper to taste.
3 Open your warm grilled buns, arrange a layer of lettuce inside each one and top with the lobster mixture.
Per serving 424 cals, 5.4g sugars, 27.7g fat (4.2g saturated), 16.2g protein, 24.6g carbs

JAPANESE GRILLED SALMON & SEAWEED SALAD
Serves 4
- 500g salmon fillet, skinned and pin-boned
- 2 tbsp low sodium soy sauce
- 2 tbsp acacia honey
- 1 tbsp togarashi seasoning
- Juice of 1 lime
- 1 tbsp black sesame seeds
- 20g dried seaweed salad or wakame, shredded (see note)
- 4 spring onions, shredded
- 1 cos lettuce, roughly torn

Dressing
- Zest of 2 limes, juice of 1
- Zest and juice of 1 orange
- 3cm piece of ginger, peeled and grated
- 1 garlic clove, crushed
- 1 tbsp low sodium soy sauce
- 1 tbsp sesame oil

1 Turn the grill up to high and line a shallow oven pan with foil. Lay the salmon skin-side down in the pan, spoon over the soy and honey and sprinkle with togarashi seasoning.
2 Cook under the grill for 15-18 minutes until sticky and the salmon flakes easily when prodded. Remove from the grill, squeeze over the lime, and set aside.
3 In a small dry frying pan, fry the sesame seeds over a medium heat until just toasted, then set aside.
4 Place the dressing ingredients in a bowl and whisk until combined. Add the seaweed and spring onion and toss to coat, then do the same with the lettuce. Divide between plates, top with the flaked salmon and a scattering of toasted sesame seeds.
Note You can buy togarashi seasoning, dried seaweed salad and wakame seaweed at japanesekitchen.co.uk.
Per serving 328 cals, 18.6g fat (3.1g saturated), 28.2g protein, 9.8g carbs, 9.2g sugars

Salmon isn't the only fish in the sea. Mackerel is abundant during its July–February season. Fry fillets until their skin is crisp to serve with a tart gooseberry sauce, or alongside a salad of thinly pared cucumber and carrot tossed with an Asian dressing. Herring is also cheap and good. Toss fillets in flour and fry in butter to serve with simple salad, or flake through cooked linguine with chopped parsley and chilli

JAPANESE GRILLED SALMON
& SEAWEED SALAD

TROUT SALAD WITH ASPARAGUS & FENNEL

KERALAN PRAWN CURRY

FIVE-SPICE SALMON TACOS WITH MINTY CUCUMBER

TROUT SALAD WITH ASPARAGUS & FENNEL

Serves 6

- 500g new potatoes, halved
- 1 fennel bulb
- 1 x 230g bunch of asparagus
- 1 tbsp dijon mustard
- Juice of 1 lemon
- Extra virgin olive oil
- 500g rainbow or sea trout, scaled and pin-boned
- 1 tsp sweet smoked paprika
- 1 x 75g bag of pea shoots
- ½ bunch of dill, chopped

1 Cook the potatoes in a large pan of salted water until tender. Drain. Shave the fennel and asparagus into a bowl of ice cold water and set aside.
2 Mix the mustard with the lemon, a pinch of salt and pepper, and top up with olive oil until tripled in volume. Set aside.
3 Season the trout, sprinkle over the paprika and rub with a little oil. Put a large frying pan on a high heat and cook the fish, skin side down, for 3-4 minutes until crisp. Flip over and cook for another minute. Transfer onto a plate, skin side up.
4 Place the asparagus and fennel in a bowl with the pea shoots, potatoes, dill and dressing. Toss together. Spread over a serving platter and flake over the trout.
Per serving 323 cals, 19.6g fat (3.1g saturated), 20.2g protein, 14.5g carbs, 2.9g sugars

KERALAN PRAWN CURRY

Serves 2

- 1 tbsp oil
- 1 onion, diced
- 1 red chilli, diced
- 2 garlic cloves, crushed
- 3cm piece of ginger, peeled and sliced
- 2 tsp turmeric
- 1 x 400ml tin of coconut milk
- 1 x 400g tin of chopped tomatoes
- 10 raw king prawns, peeled
- 1 tbsp chopped coriander

1 Heat the oil in a large pan and soften the onion for 8-10 minutes. Add the chilli, garlic, ginger and turmeric, cook for a couple of minutes, then add the coconut milk and tomatoes. Bring to the boil and simmer for 10-15 minutes, until thick. Add the prawns and cook for 5 more minutes. Garnish with coriander and serve with boiled rice.
Per serving 474 cals, 37.4g fat (27.4g saturated), 13.7g protein, 21.8g carbs, 15.1g sugars

FIVE-SPICE SALMON TACOS WITH MINTY CUCUMBER

Serves 4

- 4 x 125g salmon fillets, skin on
- 2-3 tsp five spice powder
- Olive oil
- A small bunch of mint, leaves picked and finely chopped
- ½ bunch of coriander, leaves picked, stalks finely chopped
- 150g plain fat-free yoghurt
- 1 cucumber
- 2 shallots, finely sliced
- 1 red chilli, finely sliced
- 1 tbsp white wine vinegar
- A pinch of sugar
- 4 corn or flour tortillas

1 Rub the salmon flesh (but not the skin) with the spice powder, a drizzle of oil and a pinch of salt and pepper. Heat a non-stick frying pan over a medium heat and cook the salmon skin side down until nearly cooked and the skin is crispy. Flip the fish over, remove from heat and let it finish cooking in the residual heat.
2 Meanwhile, combine the herbs and the yoghurt (reserve a few coriander leaves for serving). Peel the cucumber into ribbons, adding them to a bowl with the shallots, chilli, vinegar, sugar and a pinch of salt. Mix together with your hands to combine the flavours.
3 Place a tortilla on each plate and flake over the salmon fillets, including the crispy skin. Add a dollop of the minty yoghurt, some of the cucumber and the reserved coriander leaves.
Per serving 452 cals, 16.5g fat (2.7g saturated), 33.6g protein, 44.6g carbs, 6.8g sugars

SEMOLINA-FRIED SQUID & PRAWNS

SALT & PEPPER SEAFOOD

SEMOLINA-FRIED SQUID & PRAWNS

Serves 2

- 300g semolina flour
- 1 tbsp dried oregano
- 4 squid, cleaned and cut into diagonal strips
- 8 large whole raw prawns
- Olive oil, for shallow frying
- 3 lemons, cut into wedges, and a handful of fresh oregano, leaves picked and chopped, to serve

1 In a large bowl mix the semolina flour, oregano and 1 teaspoon each of salt and pepper. Toss through the squid and prawns until coated all over.
2 Heat some oil (enough to cover the seafood) in a pan on high heat. Add the seafood and fry it in batches. When golden, after 2–3 minutes, remove with a slotted spoon onto kitchen roll to drain. Serve with lemon wedges and oregano.

Per serving 570 cals, 17.8g fat (2.7g saturated), 44.9g protein, 62g carbs, 0g sugars

SALT & PEPPER SEAFOOD

Serves 8–10

- 2 tbsp white peppercorns
- 2 tbsp sichuan peppercorns
- 4 tsp chilli flakes
- 4 tbsp sea salt

- 150g flour
- 500g squid, cleaned
- 1.5 litres vegetable oil for frying
- A small cube of potato, to test the oil
- 500g prawns, shelled
- Jaggery (or dark brown sugar), to taste
- Lime wedges, to serve

1 With a pestle and mortar, bash the white and sichuan peppercorns to a powder. Add the chilli flakes and salt, and continue to crush. Add 2 tablespoons of the flour, crush a little more, then mix in a large bowl with the remaining flour.
2 Cut the squid open, score the insides in a criss-cross pattern and cut into bite-sized pieces. Heat the oil in a large saucepan over a medium-high heat. Place the cube of potato in the oil; once it floats and turns golden, the oil is ready.
3 Toss the squid pieces in the spiced flour mixture, shaking off any excess coating. Fry the coated squid, in batches, for 1–2 minutes until golden.
4 Once you have finished the squid, do the same with the prawns, tossing them in the flour mixture then cooking for 1 minute longer than the squid. Drain all the seafood on kitchen paper and place in a bowl. Sprinkle with a little jaggery or brown sugar and serve with lime wedges on the side.

Per serving 245 cals, 13.3g fat (1.7g saturated), 18.4g protein, 12.3g carbs, 0.2g sugars

LEMON SOLE WITH PEPPER, BUTTER BEAN & OLIVE SAUCE

Serves 4

- 4 tbsp olive oil, plus a drizzle extra
- 1 onion, finely diced
- 2 pointed sweet red peppers, deseeded and sliced
- 400g tinned chopped tomatoes
- 1 tbsp sundried tomato paste
- 50g pitted olives
- 280g tinned giant butter beans in tomato sauce
- A handful of dill, chopped
- 4 lemon soles
- 100g panko crumbs

1 For the sauce, heat half the oil in a pan and fry the onion for 5 minutes until soft. Add the peppers and fry for 2 minutes. Add the tomatoes, paste and olives; season. Bring to the boil, then simmer, covered, for 10 minutes. Add the beans and dill and heat for 1 minute. Set aside.
2 Heat the remaining oil in a non-stick frying pan and cook the fish, skin-side down. Once the skin is golden, turn the fish and fry until cooked through. Put on serving plates and pour the sauce over. Heat a drizzle of oil in the fish pan and fry the crumbs till golden. Season lightly, then scatter over the dish.

Per serving 429 cals, 14.4g fat (2.2g saturated), 33.9g protein, 44.7g carbs, 11.4g sugars

LEMON SOLE WITH PEPPER, BUTTER BEAN & OLIVE SAUCE

SEA BASS IN A BAG WITH PASTIS, FENNEL & SATSUMA

SEA BASS IN A BAG WITH PASTIS, FENNEL & SATSUMA

Recipe by Nathan Outlaw

Nathan says, "Satsumas are a memory of Christmas, and with fennel, work so well when steamed with the fish."

Serves 4

- 1 fennel bulb, trimmed and cut into 8 wedges
- 1 x 1kg sea bass, scaled, gutted and fins trimmed
- 1 shallot, finely chopped
- 1 garlic clove, finely chopped
- 75g butter, cubed
- Zest and juice of 1 satsuma
- 100ml pastis (see note)
- Green salad and boiled new potatoes, to serve (optional)

1 Preheat the oven to 220C/gas 7. You'll need an oven tray big enough for the whole bass to fit on.
2 Cut 2 pieces of greaseproof paper big enough to cover the fish completely, and lay them, one on top of the other, on a work surface. Place the fennel in the centre of paper, followed by the sea bass, shallot, garlic, butter and zest. Bring the edges of the paper over the fish, leaving an opening at the top. Pour the pastis and satsuma juice into the hole, then finish wrapping the fish. Bake in the oven for 15 minutes.
3 Serve the wrapped fish on a warmed platter. When ready, cut open the bag and serve with a green salad and boiled new potatoes on the side.
Note Pastis is an anise-flavoured aperitif. It's available in most supermarkets or you can buy it online at thedrinkshop.com.
Per serving 493 cals, 29.5g fat (10.8g saturated), 49.3g protein, 29.5g carbs, 24.2g sugars

PICKLED HERRING WITH HORSERADISH YOGHURT

Recipe by Nathan Outlaw

"The combination of herring, cucumber and horseradish works so well, I think it's one of my favourites," says Nathan of this great prep-ahead dish. "The yoghurt will last in the fridge for about a week. The fish needs 24 hours in the fridge, so start this the day before you want to eat."

PICKLED HERRING WITH HORSERADISH YOGHURT

Serves 6-8

- 8 whole herring, gutted, scaled and butterflied
- 1 tsp white peppercorns
- 1 tsp fennel seeds
- 2 bay leaves
- 250ml cider vinegar
- 2 shallots, finely sliced
- 50g fresh grated horseradish
- 2 garlic cloves, crushed
- 100g caster sugar
- 2 tsp salt
- 100ml olive oil
- 2 tbsp chopped dill
- 1 cucumber, peeled and deseeded
- 50g creamed horseradish
- 200ml thick Greek-style yoghurt
- Crusty bread, to serve (optional)

1 Arrange the herring fillets in a dish that is big enough for them to lay side by side and for the liquid to cover them. Set aside until ready to pickle.
2 To make the pickling liquid, pop the peppercorns, fennel seeds, bay leaves, vinegar, shallots, grated horseradish, garlic and sugar in a pan and place over a high heat. Bring to a simmer and leave to bubble for 2 minutes, then add the salt. Remove from the heat and set aside to cool.
3 Once cooled, pour the liquid over the herrings and place a layer of clingfilm flush to the fish so they stay submerged. Chill in the fridge for 24 hours.
4 About an hour before you're ready to serve, take the fish out of the fridge and let it come up to room temperature. Meanwhile, make the dressing. Mix 50ml of the pickling liquid with the olive oil and dill. Dice the cucumber and add to the dressing. In a separate bowl combine the creamed horseradish and yoghurt.
5 Serve the herring fillets drizzled with the cucumber dressing, with horseradish yoghurt and bread on the side.
Per serving 480 cals, 28.5g fat (7.7g saturated), 37.5g protein, 17.8g carbs, 17g sugars

LEMON SOLE WITH BROWN SHRIMP, CUCUMBER & ALMONDS

LEMON SOLE WITH BROWN SHRIMP, CUCUMBER & ALMONDS

Recipe by John Rotheram of Fifteen
Serves 1

- 20ml olive oil
- 60g butter
- 1 lemon sole (400-600g)
- Juice of 1 lemon
- ¼ cucumber, sliced 5mm thick
- 30g peeled brown shrimp
- 10g wild fennel, thinly sliced
- 10g whole almonds

1 Heat the olive oil in a frying pan over a high heat until almost smoking. Add the butter, followed by your whole fish and cook on each side for about 4 minutes, or until golden brown.
2 Once cooked, transfer the fish to a plate (keeping all the juices in the pan) and keep it warm. Return the pan to a low heat. Add the lemon juice and stir,

making a nutty brown butter. Remove the pan from the heat and add all of the remaining ingredients. Spoon this over the sole and serve.

Per serving 983 cals, 79.7g fat (35.2g saturated), 61.5g protein, 3.5g carbs, 0.9g sugars

....

JERK FISH

This Jamaican-inspired seafood dish is so fresh, spicy and so delicious.
Serves 4

- 4 whole fish (such as sea bream or red mullet), gutted and scaled
- 2 limes, cut into wedges, to serve

Jerk marinade
- 1 tbsp allspice berries
- 1 tbsp black peppercorns
- 2 bay leaves
- A large pinch of ground cloves
- ½ tbsp muscovado sugar
- 2 tbsp runny honey
- 1 tbsp picked thyme, chopped
- A few sprigs of coriander, chopped
- 2 scotch bonnet chillies, chopped
- 2 garlic cloves, finely chopped
- 3cm piece fresh ginger, peeled and finely chopped
- 2 spring onions, finely sliced
- Zest of 1 lime
- Olive oil
- 2 tbsp golden rum (optional)

Corn salsa
- 3 fresh corn on the cob
- 1 ripe mango, peeled and chopped
- 4 spring onions, finely sliced
- ½ bunch of fresh coriander, chopped
- 2 tomatoes, chopped
- Zest and juice of 2 limes

1 Lay the fish in a shallow oven dish, make 3 slashes in the flesh of each one with a sharp knife, and set aside.
2 For the marinade, pound the allspice berries, peppercorns and bay leaves in a pestle and mortar until fine. Mix in the cloves, sugar and honey, add the herbs, chillies, garlic and ginger and bash all of it together until combined.
3 Tip the mixture into a jug, add the chopped green tops of the spring onions, the lime zest, a drizzle of oil, a pinch of salt and the rum, if using. Mix well.
4 Pour the marinade over the fish and massage it in. (It's a good idea to wear rubber gloves for this!) Leave in the fridge to marinate for at least 1 hour.
5 Meanwhile, prepare the salsa. Heat a griddle pan until searing hot, and cook the corn for 5-10 minutes, turning every minute or two until the corn is evenly charred. Set aside until they're cool enough to handle, then carefully remove the kernels with a sharp knife.
6 Add the kernels to a serving bowl with the mango, spring onions, coriander and tomatoes. Season with a little salt and pepper, add the lime juice and zest, a splash of olive oil, and toss to combine. Preheat the oven to 220C/gas 7.
7 Bake the fish for 15-20 minutes, until slightly charred and cooked through. Serve each fish whole, with the corn salsa on the side and a few lime wedges for squeezing over.

Per serving 515 cals, 13.7g fat (0.7g saturated), 57.2g protein, 36.5g carbs, 20.3g sugars

JERK FISH

VIÑA MAIPO

RESERVA

Vitral

CHARDONNAY
CHILE

RESERVA

VIÑA MAIPO

Vitral

SYRAH
CHILE

RESERVA

Vitral

UNIQUE
COMPOSITION

CHILE
WWW.VINAMAIPO.COM

POULTRY

Both chicken and game birds offer succulent, tender meat that matches well with a whole host of flavours. Enjoy different cuts in a variety of ways, from wraps and salads to tray bakes and of course, a classic juicy roast

VIÑA MAIPO

PHEASANT SCHNITZEL

7 Toss the dill through the potatoes, then serve with the schnitzel, redcurrant sauce and a dollop of sour cream.

Per serving 506 cals, 22.2g fat (5.8g saturated), 34.4g protein, 45.1g carbs, 12.4g sugars

PARTRIDGE KIEV

Serves 4

- 1 garlic clove
- 75g unsalted butter, softened
- 1 small bunch of flat-leaf parsley, leaves picked and finely chopped
- 4 x 60g skinless partridge breasts
- 50g flour
- 2 eggs, beaten
- 2 handfuls of stale breadcrumbs
- Olive oil
- 1 lemon, cut into wedges, to serve
- Garden salad, to serve

1 Make a garlic butter by pounding the garlic and a good pinch of salt with a pestle and mortar until you have a paste. Add the butter and parsley and continue pounding until well mixed. Spoon the butter onto a piece of greaseproof paper and tightly roll up into a log shape, twisting each end like a Christmas cracker to seal. Place it in the fridge and leave to chill for at least 20 minutes.
2 Lay the partridge breasts, smooth side down, on a chopping board then make a small incision in the thick part of each fillet to make a little pocket.
3 Cut knobs of garlic butter off the log (you'll probably use about half of it) and stuff a slice in each pocket. Save the leftover butter for another day.
4 Preheat the oven to 200C/gas 6. Scatter the flour on a plate along with a good pinch of salt and pepper, then whisk the eggs in a shallow bowl and put the breadcrumbs in a third bowl. Dip each partridge fillet in the flour, then in the egg, then finally in the breadcrumbs, turning to coat all over.
5 Heat a glug of olive oil in a large ovenproof pan over a medium–high heat. Fry the kievs for 1–2 minutes on each side, until lightly golden. Transfer the pan to the oven and bake the kievs for 8–10 minutes, or until cooked through. Serve straight away with lemon wedges and a garden salad.

Per serving 348 cals, 20.5g fat (7.1g saturated), 27.5g protein, 14.9g carbs, 0.6g sugars

PHEASANT SCHNITZEL

Serves 4

- 600g new potatoes, any large ones halved
- Finely grated zest and juice of 2 lemons
- Extra virgin olive oil
- 1 tbsp dijon mustard
- 30g flour
- 1 egg
- 2 big handfuls of stale breadcrumbs
- 4 x 100g skinless pheasant breasts, trimmed
- 1 large bunch of dill, leaves picked and finely chopped
- 4 tbsp redcurrant jelly
- Sour cream, to serve

1 Boil the potatoes in a pan of salted water for about 12 minutes, or until tender. Drain in a colander and leave to steam dry for a few minutes, then tip them into a large bowl.

2 In a separate bowl, pour in the juice of 1 lemon, the same amount of olive oil and the mustard. Season and whisk together. Tip over the hot potatoes, toss to coat, then set aside.
3 Scatter the flour on a plate, and whisk the egg in a shallow bowl. In another bowl, mix the breadcrumbs with the lemon zest, season, then line it up next to the egg and flour.
4 Place the meat on some greaseproof paper, then cover with another sheet. Bash the breasts until flattened to roughly 5mm thick.
5 Heat a glug of olive oil in a pan over a medium-high heat. Dip each breast in the flour, then the egg, then coat in the breadcrumbs, before frying for 2-3 minutes on each side, or until cooked through and golden.
6 Remove the pheasant from the pan, turn down the heat, then pour in the remaining lemon juice to deglaze it, and stir in the redcurrant jelly.

PARTRIDGE KIEV

Though Mexican in origin, tortillas are a brilliant base for a world of hands-on dishes. For a simple lunch, wrap around strips of chicken with sliced romaine lettuce and caesar salad dressing, or use to encase chunky falafels and tzatziki. Or try pork meatballs in a tomato sauce with melting fontina cheese; shredded duck, spring onion and hoisin sauce; or a lamb, potato and pea curry with a minty raita

CHICKEN BURRITOS

CHICKEN BURRITOS

Serves 4

- 2 tomatoes, chopped
- 1 green chilli, diced
- ½ onion, diced
- Juice of ½ lemon
- 2 tbsp chopped coriander
- 4 chicken breasts, sliced into 1cm strips
- 1 tsp cumin seeds, lightly ground
- 1 tsp coriander seeds, lightly ground
- 1 tbsp oil
- 1 x 400g tin of black beans
- 4 tortillas

1 Preheat the oven to 180C/gas 4. Combine the tomatoes, chilli, onion, lemon juice and fresh coriander in a small bowl and set aside. Coat the chicken strips in the ground cumin and coriander seeds, and season.
2 Heat the oil in a frying pan over a medium heat and cook the chicken for 10-12 minutes, stirring frequently, until cooked through.
3 Meanwhile, warm the beans in a pan. Wrap the tortillas in foil and heat in the oven for 5 minutes. Lay a tortilla out and pile up with beans, chicken and tomato salsa. Wrap and serve.

Per serving 442 cals, 7.7g fat (1.5g saturated), 41.3g protein, 49.7g carbs, 3.9g sugars

CHICKEN ARRABIATA

Serves 4-6

- 4 chicken breasts
- Olive oil
- 5 red chillies
- 6 garlic cloves, finely sliced
- 1 bunch basil, leaves picked and stalks finely chopped
- 3 x 400g tins chopped tomatoes
- 10 black olives, destoned
- 600g mixed ripe tomatoes, roughly chopped
- 2 tablespoons of small capers
- A couple of handfuls of rocket
- Zest of ¼-½ lemon, to serve
- A grating of parmesan, to serve

1 Place the chicken breasts between 2 layers of greaseproof paper and, with a rolling pin, bash the chicken breasts until they're about 1cm thick. Season the chicken with salt, pepper and a little drizzle of olive oil. Rub this all over on both sides, then set aside.
2 Heat a good glug of olive oil in a medium-sized pan over a low heat. Prick 4 chillies, finely slice 4 garlic cloves and add to the pan along with the basil stalks and half of the leaves. Gently cook for about 15-20 minutes, until softened but not coloured.
3 After 20 minutes remove the basil leaves (which should be beautifully transluscent) and save them for later. Fish out the chillies, slice them open then scrape out and discard the seeds. Also scrape out the flesh and add it to the pan, discarding the skin.
4 Turn the heat up to medium and add the tinned tomatoes and remaining basil leaves, allowing the sauce to bubble away for at least 20 minutes, until it has thickened and the tomatoes have broken down. Tear up the olives and add to the sauce, along with the fresh tomatoes and most of the capers. Season to taste.
5 Place a griddle pan on a high heat and allow it to get super hot. Once hot, place the chicken breasts on the griddle and cook for a couple of minutes each side, or until golden and cooked through (the juices should run clear when the meat is pricked). Leave to rest for a couple of minutes, then slice the chicken into long strips.
6 To serve, finely slice the remaining garlic and fry it in a little olive oil along with the remaining capers until crispy. Pour the tomato sauce onto a platter and lay the chicken slices on top. Sprinkle with your garlic, capers and the leftover chilli, deseeded and finely chopped. Scatter over some lemon zest, a little grated parmesan, the rocket leaves and the beautifully transluscent basil.

Per serving 320 cals, 8.3g fat (1.4g saturated), 27.2g protein, 0.2g carbs, 0.5g sugars

CHICKEN ARRABIATA

SWEET & SPICY CHICKEN THIGHS

- 4 fresh bay leaves
- 4 tbsp white wine vinegar

Florentine potatoes
- 1.2kg red-skinned potatoes
- 6 tbsp olive oil
- 4 garlic cloves, skin on, smashed
- A few sprigs of oregano

French dressing
- ½ tsp dijon mustard
- 6 tbsp extra virgin olive oil
- 2 tbsp white wine vinegar

Salad
- 4 large handfuls of lambs lettuce
- 2 frisée, inner white leaves picked and green leaves discarded
- ½ bunch of chives

1 Mix all the marinade ingredients together in a large bowl and set aside.
2 Slash the chicken across each leg about 3 or 4 times - this will allow the heat to penetrate directly into the meat and will help it to cook faster. Place the chicken in the marinade, rubbing the flavour all over. Cover and leave to chill in the fridge for at least 12 hours.
3 Preheat the oven to 190C/gas 5. Remove the chicken from the brine and pat it dry with kitchen towel, then place in a roasting tray. Cut a lemon in half and pop it inside the chicken's cavity with the bay leaves from the brine. Cover with a double sheet of tin foil and roast in the oven for 1 hour, until golden and cooked through.
4 Meanwhile, cut the potatoes into rough 2cm cubes and toss in a large roasting tray with a good splash of olive oil, the smashed garlic and the picked oregano. Season well with sea salt and black pepper and roast alongside the chicken for about 40 minutes, or until crispy and golden.
5 After an hour, remove the chicken from the oven and finish on the barbecue, turning occasionally until beautifully coloured and crisp all over.
6 Make the French dressing by shaking up the mustard, extra virgin olive oil, vinegar, plus a pinch of sea salt and black pepper, in a jam jar. Add the salad greens to a serving bowl, drizzle over the dressing and toss to coat. Serve the chicken with the crispy potatoes and the chive salad.

Per serving 601 cals, 33.6g fat (5.9g saturated), 38.4g protein, 33.6g carbs, 4.5g sugars

SWEET & SPICY CHICKEN THIGHS
Serves 4
- 8 chicken thighs, trimmed of extra fat
- 2 onions, cut into thick rings
- ½ tbsp oil
- 100g honey
- 5 tbsp sweet chilli sauce
- 3 garlic cloves, crushed
- 1 tbsp tomato purée
- 1 tbsp white wine vinegar
- 2 tbsp soy sauce
- Juice of 3 limes, zest of 2
- Stir-fry vegetables and noodles, to serve (optional)

1 Preheat the oven to 180C/gas 4. Put the chicken and onions in a roasting tray with the oil; season and roast for 20 minutes. Meanwhile, mix together the honey, sweet chilli sauce, garlic, tomato purée, vinegar, soy, lime zest and juice. Pour it over the chicken and cook for a further 30 minutes, until the sauce is sticky and the chicken is cooked through. If the sauce is still runny, put the roasting tray over the hob and let it bubble for a few minutes. Serve with noodles and stir-fried vegetables, if you like.

Per serving 389 cals, 12.2g fat (3g saturated), 30.6g protein, 40.8g carbs, 37.5g sugars

FRENCH-STYLE CHICKEN
The best way to cook a whole chicken on the barbecue is to be safe and cook it blonde in the oven first. Then finish it on the barbecue to get that crispy, golden skin, letting the smoky flavour penetrate right through.
Serves 6
- 1.8kg chicken, free-range or organic

Marinade
- 1 onion, finely chopped
- ½ garlic bulb, smashed
- 1 small bunch of fresh rosemary, leaves picked and finely chopped

FRENCH-STYLE CHICKEN

MEXICAN CHICKEN CHILLI

MEXICAN CHICKEN CHILLI

The perfect way to warm up is with the heat of chilli. For a change, you could swap the chicken for pork.

Serves 4-6

- 1 tbsp olive oil
- 2 onions, sliced
- 4 garlic cloves, finely chopped
- ½ bunch of coriander, leaves picked, stalks finely chopped
- 1 tsp ground cumin
- ½ tsp ground coriander
- 1 whole dried chipotle chilli
- A pinch of dried chilli flakes
- 2 chicken breasts, sliced into 1cm strips
- 800g tinned chopped tomatoes
- 410g tinned black beans, drained
- 4-6 flour tortillas, to serve
- 2 gem lettuces, chopped, to serve
- Fat-free Greek-style yoghurt, to serve
- Lime wedges, to serve

Tomato salsa

- 1 red pepper
- 1 red chilli
- 4 ripe tomatoes
- 3-4 spring onions
- ½ bunch of coriander, leaves picked
- Juice of 1 lime

1 Heat the olive oil in a pan over a medium heat, then sauté the onions, garlic, coriander stalks, spices, and whole and flaked chilli for 5 minutes, until the onion is soft but not coloured.
2 Add the chicken strips and cook for a couple of minutes, then add the tinned tomatoes. Bring to the boil, then simmer, partly covered, for 35-40 minutes, until the chicken breaks apart when pressed with the back of a spoon.
3 Meanwhile, make the salsa. Place the pepper and chilli under a hot grill. Once blackened, place in a bowl, cover with cling film and set aside to cool. Chop the tomatoes, put in a colander with a pinch of salt and leave in the sink for 15 minutes to allow the salt to draw out the water from the tomatoes.
4 Peel and discard the skins from the pepper and chilli. Chop the flesh on a board along with the spring onions. Add the tomatoes and coriander and continue chopping it until you have a fine salsa. Transfer into a bowl and season to taste with black pepper and lime juice.

DUCK BREAST WITH PLUM SAUCE

5 Shred the chicken in the pan. Stir in the black beans and cook for another couple of minutes, then stir in the coriander.
6 Serve the chicken chilli in the tortillas along with chopped lettuce, a good spoonful of the salsa and a drizzle of yoghurt, with lime wedges on the side.
Per serving 547 cals, 7.4g fat (1.3g saturated), 46g protein, 69.3g carbs, 16g sugars

....

DUCK BREAST WITH PLUM SAUCE

Serves 4

- 30g butter
- 1 shallot, chopped
- 2 garlic cloves, crushed
- 3cm piece of root ginger, grated
- ½ red chilli, deseeded and chopped
- 450g plums, destoned and chopped
- 80g soft brown sugar
- 1 tbsp soy sauce
- 100ml cider vinegar
- 4 duck breasts, skin scored
- 1 cucumber, peeled and cut into batons
- 1 bunch spring onions, sliced
- Cooked rice, to serve

1 Melt the butter in a pan over a medium heat and fry the shallot, garlic, ginger and most of the chilli, until soft. Add the plums and cook for 1 minute. Stir in the sugar, soy and vinegar. Simmer with the lid on for 8-10 minutes, until the plums have cooked down and the sauce is thick.
2 Season the duck breasts on both sides and place skin side down in a dry pan. Cook over a medium heat for 3-5 minutes, until the skin is crisp. Turn over and cook for 3-5 more minutes, basting with the fat in the pan. Remove from the heat and rest for 5-10 minutes. Serve with the cucumber and spring onions, the plum sauce, the remaining chilli and a bowl of rice on the side.
Per serving 825 cals, 32.7g fat (10.4g saturated), 78.4g protein, 56.5g carbs, 55.2g sugars

CONFIT CHICKEN WITH RISOTTO BIANCO

up the skin in a hot, dry frying pan with the sage until golden. Serve with the risotto, steamed Tenderstem broccoli and a sprinkling of parmesan.

Per serving 603 cals, 39g fat (10.2g saturated), 29.8g protein, 25.7g carbs, 3.6g sugars

CHICKEN PANZANELLA
Serves 8

- 1.5kg chicken
- Olive oil
- A bunch of mixed herbs, such as sage, rosemary and thyme
- 1 ciabatta loaf (about 270g)
- 1 garlic bulb, cloves crushed
- 2kg mixed ripe tomatoes
- A bunch of basil, leaves picked
- 1 small red onion, finely sliced
- Red wine vinegar
- 100g whole black olives, destoned
- 2 tbsp baby capers
- Parmesan for shaving

1 Preheat the oven to 180C/gas 4. Rub the chicken with salt, pepper and olive oil and stuff with the herbs, reserving some of the rosemary for later.
2 Tear up the ciabatta and scatter in a roasting tin along with the crushed garlic. Place the chicken on top. Roast for 1½ hours, until cooked through and the juices run clear when pierced with a skewer. Once cooked, take it out of the oven and leave to rest.
3 Roughly chop the tomatoes. Keep half to one side and add the rest to a large bowl with half of the basil. Keep the remaining leaves for later.
4 Add the onion to the bowl along with a splash of red wine vinegar. Scrunch the whole lot together with your hands. Taste and season, if necessary.
5 Add 4 tablespoons of red wine vinegar with 2 tablespoons of olive oil, season, then stir. Add most of the baked bread to the bowl (reserving a few pieces), and toss together really well.
6 Chop up the olives and add to the bowl with the capers and remaining tomatoes, bread and basil. Mix gently and finish with a sprinkling of rosemary leaves and shavings of parmesan. Carve the chicken and serve with the panzanella.

Per serving 328 cals, 11.1g fat (2.4g saturated), 27.2g protein, 27.2g carbs, 10g sugars

CONFIT CHICKEN WITH RISOTTO BIANCO
Serves 4

- 4 chicken legs, skin on
- 8 peppercorns
- 2 red chillies, pricked
- 6 bay leaves
- A small bunch of rosemary
- 1 litre olive oil
- A few sprigs of sage

Risotto bianco

- Olive oil
- 2 sticks of celery, finely chopped
- 1 white onion, finely chopped
- 2 bay leaves
- 250g risotto rice
- 150ml white wine
- 600ml hot chicken stock
- A knob of butter
- Parmesan cheese
- Tenderstem broccoli, to serve

1 Place a large non-stick pan over a medium heat. Add the chicken legs and cook for about 5 minutes each side, or until brown all over. Place the legs into a pan with the peppercorns, chillies, bay and rosemary. Cover with the oil. Poach over the hob for around 1½ hours. Keep the chicken in the oil until ready to serve.
2 When the chicken is 30 minutes away from being done, start your risotto. Place a large saucepan over a medium heat with a glug of olive oil. Add the celery, onion and bay leaves. Cook for around 10 minutes, until soft.
3 Pour in the risotto rice and keep stirring for 2 minutes. Add the wine and continue cooking until reduced by half. Then ladle in the hot stock, stirring and making sure the liquid is absorbed by the rice before adding the next ladleful.
4 When the risotto is creamy, season and add the butter and a good grating of parmesan cheese. Set aside.
5 Finish off your chicken. Save the oil in the fridge for another time. Drain the chicken legs on kitchen paper, then crisp

CHICKEN PANZANELLA

TANDOORI CHICKEN WITH
SPICY CURRY SAUCE

TANDOORI CHICKEN WITH SPICY CURRY SAUCE

Serves 4

- 1 tbsp cayenne pepper
- 1 tbsp chilli paste
- 2 tbsp paprika
- 1 tbsp garam masala
- 1 tsp ground coriander
- 1 tsp ground black pepper
- ½ tsp turmeric
- 2 red onions, roughly chopped
- 4 garlic cloves
- 1 large piece of ginger, grated
- Juice of 1 lemon
- 200g full-fat yoghurt
- 600g skinless chicken thigh fillets
- 2 limes, 1 cut into wedges
- A handful of coriander and mint leaves, to garnish
- 1 red chilli, sliced

Pickled red onion (optional)

- 1 red onion, finely sliced
- 2 tbsp red wine vinegar

1 In a blender, purée the spices, onions, garlic, ginger and a pinch of salt. Mix with the lemon juice and yoghurt in a bowl. Smother this over the chicken, then cook on a hot griddle pan for 4-5 minutes, or until cooked through. Squeeze over lime juice to taste.
2 Cook off any remaining marinade in a frying pan for 3-4 minutes until you have a fragrant sauce.
3 To make your pickle, combine the onion, red wine vinegar and a small pinch of salt in a bowl. Leave for 5 minutes to soften, then drain off any excess liquid.
4 Serve the chicken with the sauce, pickle, herbs and chilli, alongside chappatis, raita and lime.

Per serving 336 cals, 14.4g fat (4.1g saturated), 35.6g protein, 17.2g carbs, 10.8g sugars

TUSCAN BANH MI

Makes 2 banh mi

- 2 boneless, skinless chicken thighs
- 2 garlic cloves, peeled and sliced
- 1 tsp dried oregano
- 1 tsp ground coriander
- Olive oil
- ½ lemon, sliced
- 2 small baguettes
- A handful of rocket

TUSCAN BANH MI

- A handful of mint leaves
- 1 red chilli, finely sliced

Beetroot pickle

- 1 large raw beetroot, finely sliced
- Juice of ½ lemon

Pâté

- Olive oil
- 200g chicken livers, cleaned and trimmed
- 2 garlic cloves, peeled and finely chopped
- A few sprigs of rosemary, leaves picked
- ½ small wine glass of sherry

1 Soak 4 wooden skewers in cold water and set aside. Cut the chicken thighs into 6 pieces, season, and place in a bowl with the garlic, oregano, coriander and oil. Leave to marinate overnight.
2 Make the beetroot pickle by scrunching the sliced beetroot with a pinch of salt and a squeeze of lemon juice. Set aside.
3 Remove the chicken from the marinade and feed it onto the soaked wooden skewers, with slices of lemon.
4 Meanwhile, make the pâté. Heat a little oil in a frying pan, turn up to high, then add the livers, garlic and rosemary. Cook for a couple of minutes each side, until lightly coloured but still a little pink in the middle. Add the sherry.
5 Simmer for a minute, then take off the heat and tip onto a chopping board. Chop with the garlic and rosemary.
6 Place a griddle pan over a medium heat. Slice open the baguette and toast it over the griddle. Set aside and grill the chicken. Cook for 4 minutes each side, or until cooked through and golden.
7 To assemble, spread one side of the baguette with pâté, then the beetroot. Top with 2 chicken skewers, then some rocket, mint and chilli. Squash down the top of the baguette to hold everything in place and carefully draw out the skewers.

Per serving 845 cals, 18.8g fat (5.6g saturated), 63.6g protein, 92.6g carbs, 5.7g sugars

SPAGHETTI CON RAGU DI COLOMBACCI

SPAGHETTI CON RAGU DI COLOMBACCI

Spaghetti with wood pigeon ragù
Serves 6

- 6 tbsp olive oil
- 3 wood pigeons, quartered
- 275ml red wine
- 1 large onion, finely chopped
- 2 large carrots, finely chopped
- 1 red chilli, sliced lengthways
- 1.2kg tinned tomatoes, roughly chopped, 1 tin reserved for measuring
- A bunch of basil, roughly chopped, including stalks
- 500g spaghetti

1 Heat the olive oil in a large pan and seal the pigeon. Add the red wine to the pan and cook until the liquid has evaporated.
2 Add the onion, carrot and chilli, and sweat together with the pigeon. Tip in the tomatoes and, using the empty tin, 2 tins of water, plus the chopped basil. Bring to the boil, reduce the heat, then half cover and cook for 2-3 hours on a very low heat. Check from time to time - if the meat is sticking to the pan, add another tin or so of water.
3 Cook the spaghetti according to the packet until it's al dente, then drain and mix with some of the sauce. Transfer onto a large serving dish and serve with the rest of the sauce.

Per serving 554 cals, 17.7g fat (2.1g saturated), 23g protein, 72.6g carbs, 12.1g sugars

....

AJI DE GALLINA

This deliciously warming chilli chicken dish is a classic Peruvian favourite.
Serves 4

- 25g shelled walnuts
- 1-2 red chillies, halved and deseeded, plus extra, thinly sliced, to serve
- 750g new potatoes
- Olive oil
- A large handful of black olives, destoned and torn
- A few sprigs of fresh mint, leaves picked
- 3 deboned chicken thighs, skin on
- 1 onion, finely chopped
- 2 garlic cloves, finely chopped
- 125g breadcrumbs
- 300ml milk
- 25g parmesan, finely grated
- ½ lemon, to serve (optional)

1 With a pestle and mortar, grind the walnuts until fine. Pop the chillies into a blender with 100ml of water and blitz them to a purée.
2 In a large pan of salted water, boil the potatoes for about 15 minutes until cooked through. Dry in a colander for a few minutes, then return to the pan, dress with olive oil and season.
3 Put a glug of olive oil in a small frying pan over a medium heat. Fry the olives and mint until they're lightly crispy. Add to the new potatoes.
4 Place the chicken between 2 sheets of greaseproof paper and bash with a rolling pin or a heavy pan until flattened and an even thickness. Season well, drizzle with olive oil and place in the fridge until needed.
5 In a non-stick pan over a low heat, gently fry the onion and garlic in a good glug of oil for 20 minutes, or until soft and sticky. Stir in the blitzed chilli and cook for a few more minutes before adding the breadcrumbs. Stir in the milk and cook for about 4 minutes, until the sauce thickens, adding a splash of water, if needed.
6 Stir in the ground walnuts and the grated parmesan, simmer for a further 6-7 minutes, then season and keep warm while you cook the chicken.
7 Heat a griddle pan until screaming hot and add the chicken, skin-side down. Cook for around 4 minutes, until the skin is lovely and golden, then turn and cook on the other side for 3-4 minutes until the meat is cooked through.
8 Serve the chicken on the sauce with the potato salad on the side. Add a squeeze of lemon and some extra sliced chilli, if you like.

Per serving 581 cals, 35.4g fat (9.6g saturated), 29.4g protein, 34.5g carbs, 6.6g sugars

AJI DE GALLINA

CHICKEN IN MILK

CHICKEN IN MILK

It might sound curious but cooking the bird this way makes it wonderfully moist, infused with warming flavours.

Serves 6

- 1.5kg chicken
- Olive oil
- 600ml milk
- Juice and zest of 2 lemons
- 10 garlic cloves, skin left on
- 10 peppercorns
- 4 bay leaves
- A small bunch of thyme
- Kale and chard, to serve
- Fregola pasta, cooked, to serve

1 Sit the chicken on its rear end on a chopping board and carefully, with a very sharp knife, cut down one side of the spine. Open up the chicken and lay it out on the board with the breasts facing up. Push down hard in the middle of the breasts with the palm of your hand to break the chest bone and flatten the chicken.
2 Preheat the oven to 190C/gas 5, and find a snug-fitting, deep roasting tin for the chicken. Place the roasting pan on the hob over a medium-high heat and add a generous glug of olive oil. Season the chicken generously all over and brown it in the pan for about 5-10 minutes, turning it to get an even golden colour all over.
3 Remove from the heat, transfer the chicken to a plate, and discard the oil left in the pan. This will leave a tasty, sticky goodness at the bottom of the pan which will give you a lovely caramel flavour later on. Return your chicken to the pan, then pour in the milk (two-thirds of the chicken should be submerged). Add the lemon zest and juice, then the garlic, peppercorns, bay leaves and half of the thyme.
4 Cook in the oven for 1½ hours, turning the chicken every 20 minutes, basting with the milk every time you turn it. The lemon will split the milk, making an absolutely fantastic sauce. The milk forms curds that coat the chicken and create an amazing skin as it roasts.
5 In a small pan, gently fry the remaining thyme in a splash of olive oil until crispy. To serve, cut up the chicken and divide it between your plates. Spoon over plenty

ONE-POT CHICKEN WITH ORZO

of the juice and curds, and top with the crispy thyme. Serve with kale and chard, and freshly cooked fregola pasta.

Per serving 198 cals, 9.4g fat (2.5g saturated), 27.2g protein, 0.2g carbs, 0.5g sugars

ONE-POT CHICKEN WITH ORZO

You can cook this in the oven or over the hob. You'll just need a pot large enough to hold the whole bird.

Serves 4

- 1 whole chicken
- A small bunch each of parsley, rosemary, sage and thyme, plus chopped parsley to garnish
- 4 large carrots, cut into chunks
- 3 celery stalks, cut into chunks
- 2 leeks, sliced into rounds
- 3 bay leaves
- 1.5 litres chicken or vegetable stock
- 4 handfuls of orzo (about 300g)
- Extra-virgin olive oil

1 Preheat the oven to 150C/gas 2, if using. Put your chicken in a very large saucepan or casserole with a lid. Tie the herbs together to make it easier to fish them out later. Put in with your chicken, along with the vegetables and bay leaves. Season generously.
2 Pour over the stock, topping up with water if necessary, so most of the bird is covered. To cook in the oven, start by bringing the ingredients to the boil on the hob, then cover and bake for 2½ hours. To cook on the hob, bring to the boil, cover and simmer for 2½ hours.
3 Pull the meat off the chicken – it will be moist and falling apart – and discard the carcass or use for stock. Meanwhile, cook the orzo according to the packet until tender. Divide the orzo between shallow soup bowls, then ladle over the veg, meat and stock. Scatter with the parsley and a drizzle of oil.

Per serving 713 cals, 18.6g fat (3.8g saturated), 63.9g protein, 74g carbs, 13.2g sugars

Samsung Neo Ovens

Elegant and intelligent.

With Dual Cook™ technology, Samsung Neo allows you to
simultaneously cook two different dishes, at different temperatures, for
different times, yet only takes up the space of a single oven. So you can prepare a
large roast and dessert at the same time. For every day cooking, adjust the space
to heat half the oven, using 25% less energy and saving you money.

www.samsung.com/uk/consumer/home-appliances/ovens

Warranty must be registered online within 90 days of purchase. Full terms and conditions apply. See www.samsung.com/uk/homeappliancewarranty for further details.

MEAT

Where's the beef? Right here, along with
the pork, lamb and venison. We've got all the
best cuts and accompaniments – from stews
to roasts, burgers to pies, there's a whole
range of meaty feasts to satisfy your appetite

SHANGHAI-STYLE
BRAISED PORK BELLY

fat too, but do remove it if you prefer. If you like, thicken some of the braising liquid with a little cornflour to make a sauce. Remove all fat from the sauce before thickening it.

Note Chinese rock sugar is unrefined sugar. You can buy this, and whole yellow bean sauce, at Asian grocery shops and theasiancookshop.co.uk.

Per serving 1,007 cals, 55.8g fat (18.8g saturated), 54g protein, 44g carbs, 33.6g sugars

WILD BOAR BURGERS
Serves 4

- 500g minced wild boar shoulder or belly
- 1 tbsp brown sauce, or to taste
- Worcestershire sauce, to taste
- 1 tbsp tomato sauce, or to taste
- 2 shallots, finely chopped
- 4 burger buns
- Olive oil
- 2 braeburn or cox's apples, sliced at the last minute, to serve
- 50g blue cheese, eg Colston Bassett stilton, to serve
- 30g watercress, to serve

1 Using your hands, work the mince in a bowl to break down the fat – this will act as a natural binder and help the mince stick together. Divide the meat into four, roll each piece into a ball, then flatten to roughly 1cm thick, so they're slightly larger than the buns. Pop in the fridge for 30 minutes before cooking.
2 When you're ready to cook, preheat the oven to 120C/gas ½. In a small bowl, mix the brown, Worcestershire and tomato sauces together – adding as much or as little of each, to taste – then stir in the chopped shallots and set aside.
3 Halve the buns, then pop them on a baking tray and warm in the oven for 8-10 minutes. Meanwhile, heat a drizzle of olive oil in a large non-stick pan over a medium-high heat and fry the burgers for about 4 minutes on each side, or until cooked through, seasoning as you go.
4 To build your burgers, spread the shallot sauce on the bun bases, add a few slices of apple, followed by the burger and a piece of blue cheese. Finish with watercress and serve immediately.

Per serving 412 cals, 13.3g fat (4.6g saturated), 36.1g protein, 35.7g carbs, 10.2g sugars

SHANGHAI-STYLE BRAISED PORK BELLY
Recipe by Ken Hom
Serves 6

- 1.5 kg pork belly, including bones
- 1 tbsp salt
- About 3 tbsp groundnut oil

Braising liquid

- 7.5cm piece of ginger
- 1.2 litres chicken stock
- 600ml shaoxing rice wine or dry sherry
- 150ml light soy sauce
- 150ml dark soy sauce
- 150g Chinese rock sugar (see note)
- 2 tsp five-spice powder
- 2 tsp ground white pepper
- 3 tbsp whole yellow bean sauce (see note)
- 3 tbsp hoisin sauce
- 6 spring onions

1 This joint can be cooked with its bones left in. If you get your butcher to remove them, be sure to keep them to add to the braising liquid for greater flavour. Rub the pork belly with the salt, let stand for 1 hour, then rinse. This helps to clean and firm the meat by drawing out some of the moisture. Dry with kitchen paper.
2 Heat a wok or large frying pan over a high heat. Heat the oil until slightly smoking, then brown the pork belly, rind side only, until crisp (cover to prevent splattering). Add more oil if necessary.
3 For the braising liquid, cut the ginger into 7.5 x 0.5cm slices. Place the slices in a large pot or casserole with the rest of the braising ingredients and bring to a simmer. Add the pork belly and cook slowly, covered, for 2-2½ hours or until the meat is very tender.
4 When the pork is cooked, remove from the pot and cool. (The liquid can now be cooled and frozen for reuse. Remove any surface fat before transferring it to the freezer.) Thinly slice the meat. The Chinese would serve the pork rind and

WILD BOAR BURGERS

PERSIAN-STYLE SHOULDER OF LAMB TRAYBAKE
Serves 6

- 1.5kg potatoes, chopped into wedges
- 3 red onions, quartered
- 2 fennel bulbs, each cut into 6 wedges
- 1 garlic bulb, bashed
- 3 preserved lemons, quartered
- 100g dried prunes
- 1 handful sour cherries or cranberries
- A big pinch of saffron threads
- Olive oil
- 2-2.5kg lamb shoulder, on the bone
- 4 tsp coriander seeds
- 4 heaped tsp cumin seeds
- 4 heaped tsp fennel seeds
- A few sprigs of thyme
- A few sprigs of rosemary
- Pomegranate molasses
- 2 pomegranates, seeds removed
- 1 bunch of fresh mint, leaves picked
- 75g shelled pistachios, lightly crushed

1 Preheat the oven to full whack. Pop the veg and garlic into a roasting tray with the lemons, prunes, cherries and saffron. Toss in oil, then place the lamb on top.
2 With a pestle and mortar, crush the coriander, cumin and fennel with a pinch of salt and pepper. Rub half over the lamb, setting aside the rest. Pound the thyme and rosemary with a big pinch of salt, then rub over the lamb. Poke some more rosemary into the meat.
3 Pour 100ml of boiling water in the tray and cover with tinfoil. Cook in the oven, turning the temperature down to 180C/gas 4, for about 3-4 hours.
4 Thirty minutes before the end of cooking, toss the veg, drizzle over a few tablespoons of the molasses and return to the oven. When crisp and the meat falls off the bone, it's ready. Take out of the oven and sprinkle over the remaining spices. Rest for 10-15 minutes.
5 Serve, sprinkled with the pomegranate seeds, mint and pistachios.

Per serving 846 cals, 39.6g fat (14g saturated), 47g protein, 69.5g carbs, 18.7g sugars

....

BRAZILIAN LAMB FEIJOADA
Serves 6-8

- 500g dried black beans, soaked
- 2 tbsp olive oil

BRAZILIAN LAMB FEIJOADA

- 3 onions, finely chopped
- 4 garlic cloves, finely chopped
- 2 red chillies, finely chopped
- 1 bunch of coriander, stalks finely chopped, leaves picked and chopped
- 1.5kg lamb ribs and boned shoulder of lamb, cut into 5cm pieces
- 10 merguez sausages, sliced
- 2 tsp smoked paprika
- 5 bay leaves
- 700ml passata
- Juice and zest of 1 orange

Salsa
- 1 red pepper, deseeded
- 1 green pepper, deseeded
- 4 tomatoes
- 4 spring onions, trimmed
- Juice of 1 lemon
- 1 bunch of flat leaf parsley, chopped

Pangrattato
- 75g breadcrumbs
- Olive oil
- 2 garlic cloves, finely chopped
- A few sprigs of flat leaf parsley

1 Simmer the beans in a pan of fresh salted water for 30 minutes, until tender.
2 Heat the olive oil in a large pan over a medium heat, then fry the onions, garlic, chillies and coriander stalks for 10 minutes, or until soft.
3 Add the lamb and sausages, moving around until browned, then add the smoked paprika, bay, passata, juice, and 200ml of cold water. Stir, then simmer for 1½ hours, or until the lamb falls off the bone. Add the beans and cook for a further 30 minutes, until reduced.
4 For the salsa, finely chop the peppers, tomatoes and spring onions and toss with the juice and parsley. Set aside.
5 For the pangrattato, fry the breadcrumbs in a splash of olive oil for 2 minutes. Add the remaining ingredients and fry for 5 minutes, or until golden.
6 Serve the feijoada with the salsa, pangrattato and coriander leaves.

Per serving 889 cals, 44.3g fat (17.7g saturated), 60.6g protein, 55.6g carbs, 12.1g sugars

Smart design & flexibility for the ideal roast

Once upon a time, if you wanted to roast a chicken and bake a chocolate cake at the same time, you needed two separate ovens. Twice the expense, twice the space, twice the hassle.

Well, not any more. This is because the Samsung Neo oven range has been created with Dual Cook™ technology to allow you to do just this. All you need to do is insert the specially designed insulated central shelf to create two separate compartments, each of which has its own fan, meaning that they can then be heated to different temperatures and for different lengths of time. All in the space taken up by a single oven.

The smart design opens up a world of options for the cook. On the one hand, the oven offers a huge 70-litre capacity, more than enough space to

While you cook this beef at 230C/gas 8, your Samsung Neo oven can be cooking your sides at lower temperatures. Parboiled maris pipers will turn into super roasties with an hour at 200C/gas 6. This is also the optimum temperature and time for parsnips (drizzle over some honey for the last 5 minutes to point up their sweetness) and for beetroot, roasted in foil with rosemary and a splash of balsamic vinegar

FLORENTINE ROAST

EASY ALBONDIGAS

FLORENTINE ROAST

Recipe by Dario Cecchini
Serves 8-10

- 2-2.5kg top round of beef
- A handful of sage, leaves picked
- 1 bunch of rosemary, leaves picked
- Profumo del Chianti, or fine sea salt

1 Preheat the oven to 230C/gas 8. Place the beef in a roasting pan and cook for 20 minutes without opening the oven.
2 Chop together the sage, a smaller handful of rosemary, and a few pinches of the salt. Mix in some olive oil (allow one cup of oil per kilogram of beef).
3 Remove the roast from the oven and pour over the herby liquid. Cover the pan with foil and leave to stand for half an hour for the flavours to develop.
4 To serve, slice the beef thinly and drizzle over the gorgeous steeping sauces from the pan.

Per serving 504 cals, 32.6g fat (13.6g saturated), 51.1g protein, 0.8g carbs, 0g sugars

EASY ALBONDIGAS

Serves 4-6

- 250g minced pork
- 1 egg
- A small bunch of parsley, chopped
- A pinch of paprika
- A pinch of chilli flakes
- 1 garlic clove, sliced
- Olive oil
- 2 tins of tomatoes

1 Combine the pork, egg, parsley, paprika and chilli in a bowl. Roll into 12 balls, pop them on a plate, cover and place in the fridge for 15 minutes.
2 Fry the garlic in a pan with a splash of oil over a medium heat for 1 minute. Add the tomatoes and a splash of water and cook for 15 minutes, or until thickened.
3 Add the meatballs and fry until cooked through. Add to the sauce and cook for 10 minutes over a low heat.

Per serving 161 cals, 8g fat (2.7g saturated), 16.1g protein, 6.9g carbs, 5.7g sugars

BUTTERFLIED LEG OF LAMB WITH
MEXICAN-STYLE MARINADE

6 In a large bowl, mix the spice paste with the rest of the marinade ingredients and a pinch of salt.
7 Add the butterflied lamb to the bowl and rub the marinade all over the meat. Cover and refrigerate for at least 4–6 hours, ideally overnight.
8 Remove from the fridge at least 30 minutes before you cook, so the lamb comes up to room temperature. Once your barbecue is hot, cook the meat for 40–45 minutes (medium-rare), turning it every 10 minutes or so. Transfer the lamb to a board to rest for 15 minutes.
9 Slice and serve the lamb on the board with half of the zested lemon.
Note Ancho chillies are dried poblano chillies, used in Mexican cuisine. If you can't find them at your supermarket, you can get them at souschef.co.uk.
Per serving 323 cals, 20.9g fat (5.7g saturated), 28.3g protein, 4.7g carbs, 3.5g sugars

STEAMED PORK & GINGER DUMPLINGS
Serves 4

- 1 thumb-sized piece of ginger, grated
- 1 garlic clove, grated
- 2 spring onions, finely sliced
- 1 tsp soy sauce
- 1 tsp sesame oil
- 1 head pak choi, shredded
- 120g cooked, shredded pork
- 1 packet dumpling wrappers (see note)
- 2 tbsp rice wine vinegar
- ½ red chilli, very finely sliced
- 1½ tsp golden caster sugar

1 Mix the ginger, garlic, spring onions, soy sauce, sesame oil, pak choi and shredded pork together in a bowl. Place a heaped teaspoon of the mix into the centre of each dumpling wrapper, then use a dampened finger to seal them.
2 Place the dumplings in a steamer and steam for about 4–5 minutes, until cooked through. Meanwhile, whip together a quick dipping sauce by combining the vinegar, chilli and sugar in a bowl. Serve the dumplings in the steamer with the sauce alongside.
Note You can buy dumpling wrappers from theasiancookshop.co.uk.
Per serving 120 cals, 2.6g fat (0.7g saturated), 11g protein, 12.3g carbs, 2.6g sugars

BUTTERFLIED LEG OF LAMB WITH MEXICAN-STYLE MARINADE
This leg of lamb is butterflied for quicker cooking on the barbecue.
Serves 8

- 1 x 2kg leg of lamb
- 2 dried ancho chillies (see note)
- ½ tsp black peppercorns
- 1 tsp pink peppercorns
- 2 tsp fennel seeds
- 1 tsp coriander seeds
- 1 lemon, zested
- 1 tsp sweet smoked paprika
- 1 bunch of oregano, leaves picked
- 6 tbsp olive oil
- 4 garlic cloves, crushed
- 2 red chillies, finely sliced
- 2 tbsp red wine vinegar
- 1 x 500g tub of fat-free Greek yoghurt

1 If you can, prepare your lamb the day before you want to cook it. Using a sharp knife, carefully cut down the lamb leg to expose the bone.
2 Keeping your knife as close to the bone as possible, cut along one edge to completely reveal it. Cut right around the bone, then remove.
3 Lay the lamb flat on a chopping board, skin-side down. With your knife, make an incision halfway into the flesh on each side, where the meat is thicker, then open it out like a book. You should now have a flat piece of lamb of more or less even thickness.
4 Soak your dried chillies in a bowl of hot water for 10 minutes. In a small frying pan over a medium heat, dry-toast the black and pink peppercorns, fennel and coriander seeds for 30 seconds, until they begin to pop and smell delicious.
5 Remove the softened chillies from the soaking water and transfer to a spice grinder or small food processor. Add the toasted spices and a splash of the soaking water, then blitz to a fine paste.

STEAMED PORK & GINGER DUMPLINGS

BARBECUE RIBS

LAMB DAUBE

Serves 6

- Olive oil
- 1kg boneless lamb neck and shoulder, trimmed and cut into 1.5-2cm chunks
- 5 streaky bacon rashers, chopped
- 1 large onion, roughly chopped
- 2 garlic cloves, finely sliced
- 2 celery stalks, roughly chopped
- 1 small bunch of rosemary, leaves picked and finely chopped
- 2 tbsp tomato purée
- 1 tbsp flour
- 200ml red wine
- 500ml lamb stock
- 1 bay leaf
- 1 dried bouquet garni
- 5 small carrots, tops on
- Zest of ½ large orange, peeled into thick strips
- A handful of baby new potatoes, scrubbed, half cut into chunks
- 1 small bunch of flat leaf parsley, leaves picked and roughly chopped
- Savoy cabbage, steamed then shredded, to serve
- Sourdough bread, to serve

1 Preheat your oven to 130C/gas ½. Heat a splash of olive oil in a large ovenproof pan over a medium heat. Add the lamb in batches and brown all over, then remove from the pan and set aside on a plate.
2 Tip away the excess fat from the pan, then fry the bacon, onion, garlic, celery and rosemary for 5-10 minutes or until soft. Add the purée, flour and red wine, and mix to form a paste with the gooey bits of cooked vegetables and bacon.
3 Add the lamb, along with the stock, bay leaf, bouquet garni, carrots and orange zest. Place the lid on and cook in the oven for 4 hours.
4 When the daube has about half an hour of cooking time to go, add the potatoes. When the time is up, check they're tender - if not, return to the oven for a few more minutes.
5 Before serving, remove the bouquet garni and sprinkle over the parsley leaves. Serve the daube with savoy cabbage and a lovely chunk of sourdough bread to dunk in the rich, meaty sauce.
Per serving 483 cals, 18.5g fat (7.6g saturated), 33.9g protein, 33.2g carbs, 12.3g sugars

BARBECUE RIBS

Serves 4-6

- Olive oil
- 2 racks of pork loin back ribs (about 1.6kg)
- Rocket and watercress, to serve

Marinade

- 1 red chilli
- A thumb-sized piece of ginger
- 2 garlic cloves
- 150ml apple juice
- 100ml white wine vinegar
- 2 heaped tbsp tomato ketchup
- 1 tbsp dijon mustard
- 100ml light soy sauce
- 100g soft brown sugar

1 Preheat the oven to 200C/gas 6. Drizzle a little olive oil over the ribs, season with salt and black pepper and rub all over to coat.
2 Make the marinade. De-seed and finely chop the chilli, peel and grate the ginger and garlic then place them all in a medium pan along with the apple juice, white wine vinegar, tomato ketchup, mustard, soy sauce and brown sugar.
3 Whisk the ingredients together and place the pan over a medium heat. Stir well until the sugar dissolves, then simmer for 10-15 minutes, or until the sauce has thickened.
4 Put the ribs in a roasting pan, brush with the marinade and cover with foil. Cook in the oven for 1 hour 15 minutes, until the meat pulls away from the bone.
5 Baste the ribs with the marinade after 30 minutes. After 1 hour, remove the foil then baste and cook, uncovered, for the final 15 minutes, basting halfway through. Once your barbecue is hot, transfer the ribs to it. Cook over a low-medium heat for 5-10 minutes.
6 Transfer the ribs to a board and cut them up. Serve with handfuls of rocket and watercress on the side.
Per serving 737 cals, 50.4g fat (17.9g saturated), 54.1g protein, 16.4g carbs, 15.2g sugars

PORK BELLY BUNS

PORK BELLY BUNS
Serves 20 (makes 40 buns)
- 200g caster sugar
- 1 tsp black peppercorns
- 3 star anise
- A bunch of spring onions, sliced
- 2kg pork belly, skin scored
- 2 punnets of interesting cresses, to serve
- 2 red chillies, sliced, to serve
- A range of sauces, such as hoisin, BBQ, ketchup and brown, to serve

Wheat buns
- 2 x 7g sachets dried yeast
- 1kg strong white bread flour, plus extra for rolling
- 1 tsp baking powder
- ¾ tsp bicarbonate of soda
- 2 tbsp sea salt
- 120g butter, melted
- Olive oil

Cucumber pickle
- 1 cucumber
- 1 tbsp sugar
- 100ml rice wine vinegar

1 Make your buns the day before. Put the yeast in a large bowl with 450ml warm water and leave for a few minutes. Mix in the flour, baking powder, bicarbonate of soda, salt and melted butter, then knead for 10 minutes. Place in an oiled bowl, cover and leave to prove for 2 hours.
2 Once the dough has doubled in size, knock it back on a floured surface. Split in half, then roll each into equal-sized logs. Cut each into 20 small, equal pieces. Roll each piece into a ball and place on a lined baking sheet. Cover and leave to prove again for 30-45 minutes.
3 When the buns have risen, knock each back, then roll into oval shapes about 12cm long. Coat a chopstick with a little oil, place in each bun and fold it over.
4 Place a bamboo steamer on a pan over a medium heat and line with greaseproof paper. Steam the buns (in batches) for 10-12 minutes, until light and fluffy. Leave to cool, cover and chill overnight.
5 Marinate the pork overnight by mixing the sugar, peppercorns, star anise and a good pinch of salt in a bowl. Add the pork, then cover with water. Turn to coat, then cover and chill overnight.
6 When ready to cook, preheat the oven to 150C/gas 2. Transfer the pork to a roasting tin with the marinade and cover

KALE & SAUSAGE STEW

tightly with tin foil. Cook gently for 2½-3 hours, or until tender but not coloured. Remove the meat to cool, leaving the marinade in the pan.
7 Put the pan of marinade on the hob over a medium-high heat for 20-25 minutes, or until syrupy. Cut the cooled pork into 10 slices, 1cm thick, return to the marinade and set aside.
8 For the pickle, score the cucumber with a fork, all the way round. In a serving bowl, dissolve the sugar in a splash of boiling water, and top with the vinegar. Slice the cucumber into rounds, add to the vinegar and leave to marinate.
9 Place a pan over a high heat and prepare your steamer. Fry the pork for 5-10 minutes, turning halfway, until golden, then cut into quarters. Steam the buns for 2 minutes, then assemble with the pork, pickle, spring onions, cress and chilli. Serve with the sauces.
Per serving 792 cals, 59.1g fat (22.6g saturated), 16.7g protein, 47.3g carbs, 11.4g sugars

KALE & SAUSAGE STEW
Serves 4
- 1 onion, sliced
- 2 garlic cloves
- 1 tsp fennel seeds
- ½ tsp crushed chillies
- 3 strips of lemon zest
- 1 bay leaf
- 6 sausages, chopped
- 1½ tbsp flour
- 1 x 400g tin chopped tomatoes
- 500ml vegetable stock
- A large handful of kale, chopped

1 Fry the onion in a little olive oil until softened. Add the garlic, spices, zest and bay and cook for 1-2 minutes. Toss the sausages in flour, add to the pan and cook until browned. Pour in the tomatoes and stock and simmer for 20 minutes. Add the kale and cook for 5 minutes.
Per serving 334 cals, 22.8g fat (8g saturated), 13.3g protein, 20.3g carbs, 7.1g sugars

STEAK & KIDNEY PIE

- 3 garlic cloves, finely chopped
- 3 green chillies, finely chopped
- ½ tsp turmeric
- 1 tsp cayenne
- 2 tsp ground cumin
- 2 tsp ground coriander
- 1 tsp chilli power
- 4 cloves
- 3 cardamom pods
- 1kg lamb neck fillet, cut into chunks
- 5 medium tomatoes, quartered
- 1 cinnamon stick
- 2 bay leaves
- ½ tsp garam masala
- 1 bunch of fresh coriander, leaves picked and chopped
- Pilaf rice and mint yoghurt, to serve

STEAK & KIDNEY PIE
Serves 6

- 40g plain flour, plus extra for dusting
- 1.2kg topside of beef, cut into 2cm pieces
- Olive oil
- 200g ox or lamb kidney, cleaned and quartered
- 2 red onions, sliced
- 2 rosemary sprigs, leaves picked
- 2 bay leaves
- 2 beef stock cubes, crumbled
- Worcestershire sauce
- 250g puff pastry
- 1 egg, beaten

1 Season the flour in a bowl, then toss the beef in to coat. Fry in batches in oil over a high heat until browned, then set aside. Toss the kidneys in the flour and add to the beef. Lower the pan heat to medium and fry the onion and rosemary. Once coloured, stir in the remaining flour, then the meat. Add the bay and stock. Pour in 1 litre of boiling water, a splash of Worcestershire sauce and bring to the boil, then simmer, part covered, for 2 hours. Season and add more water if needed. Leave to cool.
2 Preheat the oven to 200C/gas 6. On a floured surface, roll out the pastry to 4mm thick. Spoon the filling into a shallow 24cm pie dish, brushing the edge with egg. Cover with the pastry. Trim, crimp the edges and pierce two holes in the top. Brush with egg and bake for 25-30 minutes, until golden.

Per serving 645 cals, 38.5g fat (16.5g saturated), 51.7g protein, 32.2g carbs, 3.5g sugars

NORTH INDIAN LAMB CURRY
Serves 6

- Rapeseed oil
- 3 onions, finely sliced
- 1 thumb-sized piece of ginger, finely chopped

1 Preheat the oven to 180C/gas 4. Heat the oil in a casserole dish over a medium heat, then fry the onions and ginger until golden. Add the garlic and chilli and fry for another 2 minutes, then stir in all the spices, except for the cinnamon stick and garam masala.
2 After 5 minutes, toss in the lamb. Fry for about 10 minutes, until coloured, then stir in the tomatoes, cinnamon and bay. Cover with the lid and pop in the oven for 1½-2 hours, or until the meat starts to fall apart.
3 Serve sprinkled with the garam masala and coriander, with the rice and yoghurt.

Per serving 481 cals, 33.4g fat (14.1g saturated), 33g protein, 10.5g carbs, 7.2g sugars

NORTH INDIAN LAMB CURRY

LEG OF LAMB WITH AMAZING GRAVY

Serves 8

- 2.5-3kg leg of lamb
- 4 unpeeled red onions, halved
- 2 garlic bulbs, cloves separated and bashed

Herby butter
- 100g unsalted butter, softened
- ½ bunch of thyme, leaves picked
- ½ bunch of rosemary, leaves picked

Gravy
- 3 tbsp plain flour
- A good glug of port
- 1 litre hot organic chicken stock

Celeriac mash
- 1 celeriac, cut into 3cm chunks
- 1kg potatoes, cut into 2cm cubes
- A glug of extra virgin olive oil
- 1 whole nutmeg, for grating

Mint sauce
- 1 big bunch of fresh mint, leaves picked and chopped
- 2 tbsp red wine vinegar
- 1 tbsp soft brown sugar

1 Preheat the oven to 220C/gas 6. Score the lamb all over, ½cm apart and 3mm deep, to give it a gnarly, crispy surface and a blushing centre.
2 For the herby butter, put the butter, thyme and rosemary into a blender, season, then blitz. Set aside.
3 Arrange the onions and garlic in a large roasting tray. Smear the herby butter all over the lamb, then pop the meat on top of the veg. Roast in the oven for 10 minutes for every 450g of lamb, then add another 20 minutes at the end, for blushing meat.
4 Meanwhile, boil the celeriac and potatoes for 15-20 minutes, or until soft. Drain, allow to steam dry, then mash with a good glug of olive oil and season well with a little grated nutmeg and some salt and pepper.
5 When the lamb is cooked, rest for at least 10 minutes. Make the gravy. Set aside half a red onion to make the mint sauce, then squash the rest into the tray. Stir in the flour, a glug of port and the stock, and place over a high heat to reduce, stirring continuously. Pass through a sieve and keep hot.
6 For the mint sauce, pop the reserved onion half out of its skin, finely chop together with the mint, then mix in a

bowl with the vinegar and sugar. Take everything to the table and dig in!

Per serving 535 cals, 26.6g fat (12.9g saturated), 34.8g protein, 35.7g carbs, 8.6g sugars

VENISON STEW

VENISON STEW

Serves 8

- Olive oil
- 2 onions, finely chopped
- A few rosemary sprigs, leaves picked and chopped
- 1kg venison neck, cut into chunks
- 200g baby onions, peeled
- 2 celery stalks, finely chopped
- A good glug of balsamic vinegar
- 500ml dark beer
- 500ml beef stock
- 300g mixed wild mushrooms
- ½ bunch of thyme, leaves picked
- Seasonal greens, to serve

1 Preheat the oven to 180C/gas 4. Place a casserole dish over a medium heat and add a glug of olive oil. Tip in the chopped onion and rosemary and fry for 5-10 minutes, until golden. Transfer to a bowl.
2 Return the dish to the heat, add the venison and cook, stirring occasionally, for 15 minutes, or until the meat has browned and the juices have caramelised. Add the onions and celery and cook for a further 5-10 minutes, until the veg have softened. Pour in the vinegar, beer and stock and bring to the boil. Season well, then cover with a piece of baking parchment, followed by the lid, and transfer to the oven for 2 hours.
3 Heat a glug of oil in a pan on a medium heat, and fry the mushrooms and thyme for 10 minutes, or until any liquid has evaporated and they're turning brown.
4 After 2 hours, stir through the mushrooms and onions and return to the oven for a further 30 minutes. Serve with some fresh seasonal greens.

Per serving 270 cals, 7.4g fat (1.8g saturated), 32g protein, 10.7g carbs, 8.5g sugars

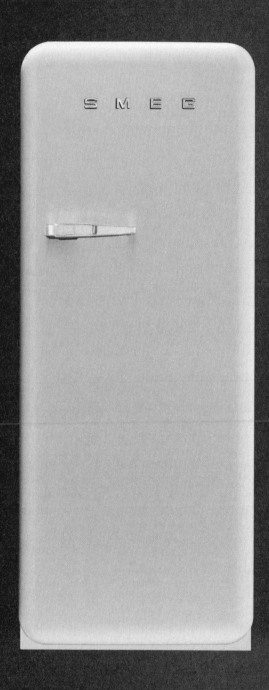

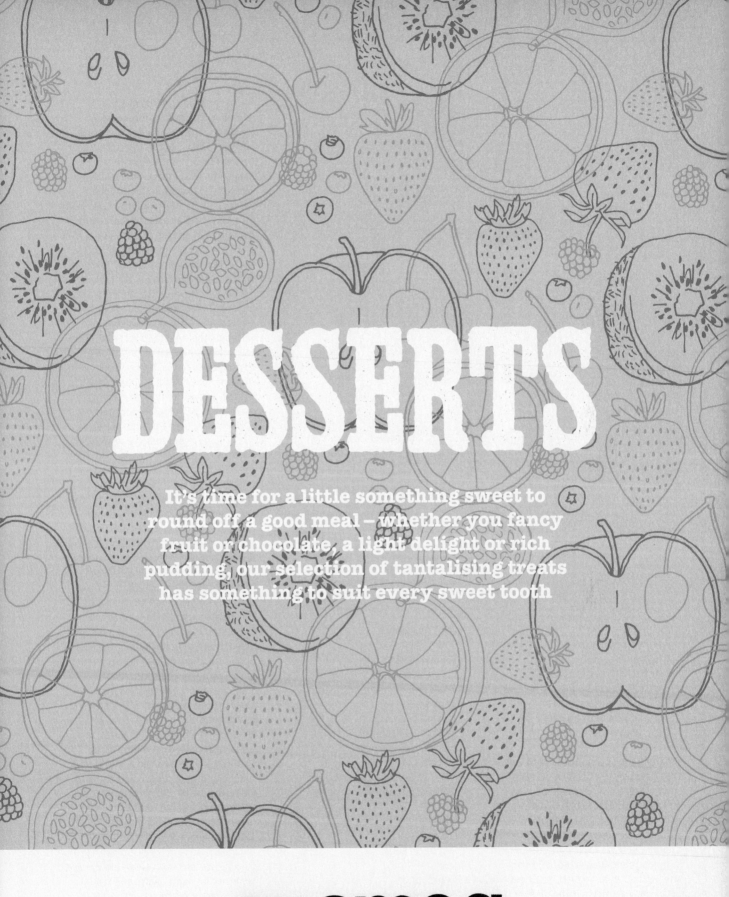

DESSERTS

It's time for a little something sweet to round off a good meal – whether you fancy fruit or chocolate, a light delight or rich pudding, our selection of tantalising treats has something to suit every sweet tooth

smeg
technology with style

ROASTED NECTARINES WITH
AMARETTI & ICE CREAM

ROASTED NECTARINES WITH AMARETTI & ICE CREAM

Serves 4

- 4 nectarines, quartered
- 1 tsp fennel seeds
- 2 tbsp golden caster sugar
- Zest and juice of 1 orange
- 4 scoops of vanilla ice cream
- 2 crushed amaretti biscuits
- 1 tsp runny honey

1 Preheat the oven to 180C/gas 4. Put the nectarines in a roasting dish and scatter over the fennel seeds, sugar and zest and juice. Bake for 10–15 minutes until the nectarines have softened and are beginning to colour slightly. Set aside to cool, then arrange in sundae glasses with the ice cream and crushed amaretti biscuits. Drizzle with honey and serve immediately.

Per serving 188 cals, 5.9g fat (3.1g saturated), 4g protein, 31.8g carbs, 31.2g sugars

CHRISTMAS COLCHESTER PUDDING

Serves 12

- 100g tapioca
- 600ml milk
- Vanilla extract
- 150g caster sugar
- Finely grated zest of 1 clementine
- 3 egg yolks
- 1 vanilla pod
- 200ml double cream
- 100g flaked almonds
- 50g icing sugar
- Finely grated zest of 2 oranges
- Gold leaf, to garnish

Berry compote
- 500g mixed fresh berries
- Cointreau
- 50g caster sugar

Meringue
- ⅓ cup water
- 300g caster sugar
- 5 egg whites
- Natural pink food colouring (optional)

1 Soak the tapioca in the milk in a saucepan for 1 hour before cooking. Place the pan over a medium heat and add the vanilla, 100g of the caster sugar, clementine zest and a pinch of salt. Simmer for 20 minutes, until thickened. Turn off the heat and allow to cool.
2 Heat 200ml water in another saucepan over a low heat. In a heat-proof bowl mix the egg yolks and remaining sugar and place over the simmering water. Whisk the yolks and sugar until thick. Take off the heat and fold through the tapioca.
3 In another bowl, whisk the cream until it forms soft peaks and fold through the tapioca. Allow to cool completely.
4 Preheat the oven to 180C/gas 4. Place the almonds in a colander and rinse under cold water. Drain and tip into a bowl with the icing sugar and orange zest, tossing to coat. Spread over a lined baking tray and bake for 10 minutes, until golden. Allow to cool, then chop into pieces.
5 For your compote, mix the berries and sugar in a saucepan. Cook over a low heat for 10 minutes, so the berries are cooked but still hold their shape. Remove with a slotted spoon and set aside. Simmer the pan of juice over a medium heat until reduced to a light syrup. Leave to cool.
6 Whisk the egg whites in a mixer on high until they form stiff peaks. In a saucepan mix the sugar and water over a high heat. Add the sugar thermometer to the pan. Brush the edges of the pan to release the excess sugar crystals. When the temperature reaches 110C turn the heat down to low, then slowly let it come back up to 120C. Take the pan off the heat and allow the bubbles to settle.
7 Set the mixer speed to slow then slowly pour the syrup into the egg white in a constant stream. Let the mixer continue for a further 10 minutes on a slow speed. The egg whites should look thick and glossy. Add a few drops of food colouring, if using, and spoon into piping bags with a 10mm plain nozzle.
8 Spoon a few berries and a little syrup in the base of the serving dishes. Top with the tapioca. Pipe the meringue around the edge of the dish, then use a cook's blow-torch to set and colour. Place some berries in the centre and scatter over flaked the almonds and gold leaf.

Per serving 360 cals, 13.1g fat (5.4g saturated), 6.3g protein, 57.5g carbs, 49.3g sugars

CHRISTMAS COLCHESTER PUDDING

STRAWBERRIES IN MOSCATEL WITH ANISE BISCUITS

Grown-up treat

Spirits and liqueurs can play a pivotal role in your after-dinner sweet fix. Experiment with sweet sherries or dessert wine, as used in the recipes below, or creamy spirits like nutty Frangelico, or the cherry-hit of Grand Marnier. Try pouring a shot of Amaretto and another of espresso over vanilla ice cream for a classic affogato.

HELADO DE PASAS DE MALAGA (MALAGA RAISIN ICE CREAM)

STRAWBERRIES IN MOSCATEL WITH ANISE BISCUITS

Recipe by Sam and Sam Clark
Serves 8 (makes about 40 biscuits, so you'll have some left over)

- 800g strawberries, hulled and halved
- 400ml moscatel malaga wine or sweet sherry
- 1 heaped tbsp icing sugar

Anise biscuits

- 170g butter
- 170g sugar
- 170g flour
- 3 tbsp finely ground almonds
- 1 tbsp ground anise
- 1 tbsp brandy
- 3 egg whites
- 100g flaked almonds
- 100g granulated sugar

1 In a bowl, mix the strawberries with the moscatel and add a little icing sugar to taste. Set aside in the fridge to macerate for a few hours.
2 Preheat the oven to 160C/gas 3. Cream the butter and sugar together until light and fluffy, then beat in the flour, ground almonds and anise. Slowly add the brandy and egg whites.
3 Dollop teaspoons of the dough onto a lined baking tray about 10cm apart. Use the back of your spoon to flatten the biscuits into discs about 3cm in diameter.
4 Sprinkle liberally with the flaked almonds and sugar, then bake for 20 minutes until evenly golden and crisp. Spoon the strawberries into bowls, pour over the moscatel syrup and serve each bowl with two anise biscuits.
Per serving 300 cals, 10.9g fat (4.7g saturated), 4.2g protein, 31g carbs, 24.8g sugars

HELADO DE PASAS DE MALAGA

Malaga raisin ice cream
Recipe by Sam and Sam Clark
Serves 8 (makes just over 1 litre)

- 600ml double cream
- 300ml semi-skimmed milk
- 1 small cinnamon stick
- 1 vanilla pod
- 7 egg yolks
- 85g sugar
- 100g raisins, soaked in 100ml Pedro Ximenez sherry

1 Put the cream, milk and cinnamon in a large saucepan. Split the vanilla pod lengthways, scrape the seeds into the pan and place over a low heat. Beat the egg yolks and sugar together for 5-10 minutes, until pale and thick.
2 Once the cream mixture has reached just below boiling point, gradually whisk a little into the egg mixture to loosen it, then pour this back into the pan of cream mixture, scraping the bowl out with a spatula. Whisk well and return to a low heat, stirring constantly. Heat gently to cook the egg but be careful not to curdle it. Once the mixture thickens, and just before it bubbles, remove from the heat, pour into a bowl and place in a sink of iced water. Once cool, remove the vanilla pod and cinnamon stick.
3 Churn the mixture in an ice cream machine (in batches, if necessary), adding the raisins and sherry towards the end. If you don't have an ice cream machine, freeze the mixture in a freezer-proof container and stir every 30 minutes to prevent crystallisation – this will also help to distribute the raisins evenly. This process will take about 2 hours, depending on the temperature of your freezer. Serve with a glass of chilled Pedro Ximenez on the side, or pour it over your ice cream.
Per serving 177 cals, 115g fat (8.9g saturated), 2.1g protein, 8.3g carbs, 8.1g sugars

SWISS MERINGUES

Peppermint meringue filling
- 275g caster sugar
- 4 egg whites
- ½ tsp cream of tartar
- A few drops of pure peppermint extract

Chocolate topping
- 100g 70%-cocoa chocolate, broken into pieces
- 1 tbsp vegetable oil

1 Beat the butter and sugar until pale and fluffy. Whisk in half the beaten egg and the vanilla extract, then stir in the flour and cocoa. Divide the mixture in half, shape each into balls, wrap both in clingfilm, then chill until firm.
2 Preheat the oven to 180C/gas 4, and grease and line a baking sheet. Dust a work surface with icing sugar and roll out 1 batch of dough to 5mm thick. Cut out rounds using a 5cm cutter, then bake for 10 minutes. Cool on the baking sheet, then transfer to a wire rack. Repeat with the second batch.
3 To make the filling, place the sugar, egg whites, cream of tartar and 1½ tablespoons of water in a bowl. Beat with an electric whisk until fluffed up. Place the bowl over a pan of simmering water set over the lowest heat possible, and continue beat for 10-12 minutes, until stiff peaks form. Remove from the heat, add a few drops of peppermint extract and beat until the meringue has thickened even more.
4 Fit a 1cm plain nozzle to a piping bag and fill the bag with the peppermint meringue. Pipe onto the biscuits in an upward spiral, leavng a small border around the edge – aim for a swirl around 3-4cm tall. Place the biscuits in the fridge while you make the topping.
5 Place the chocolate pieces and oil over a pan of simmering water, stirring until the chocolate has melted, smooth. Transfer to a bowl and leave to cool at room temperature for 10 minutes.
6 To finish the teacakes, hold the chilled biscuits by the base and gently dip the meringue into the melted chocolate, swirling. Or, place the biscuits on a wire rack with greaseproof paper underneath and drizzle over the chocolate. Chill the biscuits for a few hours, then serve.

Per serving 94 cals, 4g fat (2.3g saturated), 1.4g protein, 12.9g carbs, 10.1g sugars

SWISS MERINGUES
Makes 8
- 4 egg whites
- 250g caster sugar
- ½ tsp coffee essence
- Seeds of ½ vanilla pod
- 1 tsp rosewater
- A few drops of natural pink food colouring
- 3 cardamom pods, seeds ground
- 1 tbsp pistachios, chopped

1 Preheat the oven to 110C/gas ¼. Bring a pan of water to the boil and place a bowl over it. Add the egg whites and whisk until lightly frothy. Add the caster sugar in four batches, whisking in the next batch only once the mixture has reached stiff peaks.
2 Remove the bowl from the pan and keep whisking until the mixture cools down and the meringue is shiny.
3 Divide the meringue between four bowls. Fold the coffee essence through one and the vanilla seeds through another. Fold the rosewater and food colouring through the third mixture, then fold the cardamom seeds and half the pistachios through the last batch.
4 Dollop onto a baking tray, topping the cardamom meringues with the remaining pistachios, and bake for 1½-2 hours unti they can be peeled off the baking tray without breaking. Serve with whipped cream.

Per serving 142 cals, 0.7g fat (0.1g saturated), 2.1g protein, 31.9g carbs, 31.6g sugars

MINT CHOC TEACAKES
Makes about 40
- 110g butter, softened
- 100g caster sugar
- 1 egg, beaten
- 1 tsp vanilla extract
- 150g flour
- 30g cocoa powder
- Icing sugar, for dusting

MINT CHOC TEACAKES

BRIOCHE BREAD & BUTTER PUDDING WITH CLEMENTINES

CREMA CATALANA

CHOCOLATE CHILLI MOUSSE

BRIOCHE BREAD & BUTTER PUDDING WITH CLEMENTINES

Serves 8

- 200g vine fruit
- Zest and juice of 2 clementines
- 400g brioche, sliced
- 70g soft butter
- 150g marmalade
- 260ml whole milk
- 100ml double cream
- 50g golden caster sugar
- 3 eggs
- Seeds of 1 vanilla pod
- 1 tsp ground cloves
- 1 tbsp demerara sugar

1 Preheat the oven to 180C/gas 4. Mix the fruit, zest and juice in a saucepan, bring to the boil, then set aside.
2 Spread the brioche with butter and marmalade and cut into triangles.
3 In a jug, whisk the milk, cream, sugar, eggs, vanilla and cloves. Layer the brioche and fruit in an ovenproof dish. Coat with the liquid, sprinkle with demerara sugar and bake for 20 minutes.
Per serving 516 cals, 23.6g fat (12g saturated), 8.7g protein, 69.9g carbs, 50.2g sugars

CREMA CATALANA

Serves 6

- 500ml whole milk

- Zest of ½ orange
- Zest of ½ lemon
- ½ cinnamon stick
- 1 vanilla pod, split lengthways
- 7 egg yolks
- 95g sugar, plus 6 tbsp extra, to serve
- 10g cornflour

1 Add the milk, zests, cinnamon and vanilla pod to a saucepan and gently bring to the boil. Remove from the heat and allow to infuse for 15 minutes.
2 Meanwhile, whisk the egg yolks with the sugar and cornflour until pale and creamy. Pass the milk through a sieve and discard everything else. Return the milk to the pan over a medium heat. Just before it boils, slowly add the egg mixture, whisking continuously until it has thickened, about 7 minutes.
3 When the mixture is thick enough to coat the back of a wooden spoon, remove from the heat and pour into individual dishes or ramekins. Cover each serving with a disc of greaseproof paper to prevent a skin from forming, and let it cool before placing in the fridge.
4 To serve, remove the greaseproof paper, sprinkle 1 tablespoon of sugar over each crema and caramelise with a blowtorch. Alternatively, place the sugared cremas on a tray under a preheated gas grill for a few minutes, until the sugar turns dark brown. Allow

the sugar to harden, then serve.
Per serving 261 cals, 9.6g fat (4.3g saturated), 6.7g protein, 36.7g carbs, 34.3g sugars

CHOCOLATE CHILLI MOUSSE

Serves 4-6

- 200g 70% cocoa chilli-flavoured chocolate
- 400ml double cream
- 1 egg white
- A pinch of dried red chilli flakes

1 Pour a little water into a medium-sized pan and place it over a medium heat. Break up the chocolate, then put it into a large heatproof bowl and leave it to melt over the pan of water, taking care not to let the water boil.
2 Once melted, remove from the heat and set aside to cool. In another bowl, whisk the double cream until firm. In a third bowl, whisk the egg white until it forms soft peaks. Once the chocolate has cooled, fold it into the cream, then add the egg whites, carefully folding it all together until combined.
3 Divide the mixture among your glasses or bowls and place in the fridge to set for 20-30 minutes. Before serving, sprinkle with a few chilli flakes for an extra kick.
Per serving 497 cals, 47.4g fat (29.7g saturated), 3.9g protein, 12g carbs, 10.3g sugars

Instead of ice cream, try making Sicilian-style granitas. Make a fruit syrup (two parts water to one sugar), then add your pulped fruit. Pour into a shallow tray, pop in the freezer, and scrape with a fork before it freezes to make crystals. Most fruit will work: try mango and lime; blueberry; or watermelon

POIRES BELLE HELENE

POIRES BELLE HELENE

Serves 4

Ice cream
- 300ml full fat milk
- 300ml double cream
- 125g golden caster sugar
- 1 vanilla pod
- 3 egg yolks

Poached pears
- 75g golden caster sugar
- 1 cinnamon stick
- Peeled zest of 1 small lemon
- 4 firm, nearly ripe pears

Chocolate sauce
- 75ml double cream
- 100g 70% dark chocolate, chopped

1 Prepare a water bath for your ice cream – a deep roasting tray is perfect. Fill it two-thirds full with iced water.
2 Combine the milk, cream and half the sugar in pan. Split the vanilla pod in half, scrape out the seeds, then cut the pod into 3 and add the lot to the pan. Stir over a low-medium heat until the sugar has dissolved and the mixture is just below boiling point.
3 In a bowl, whisk together the egg yolks and the remaining sugar with an electric whisk until pale and thick. Add the hot milk mixture to the bowl, stirring well to combine. Pour the mixture back into the pan and place over a very low heat, stirring continuously, until the mixture thickens slightly and coats the back of a spoon – this will take 6–8 minutes.
4 Tip the custard into a heatproof bowl and sit it in the water bath, taking care no water spills into it. Allow it to cool to room temperature, stirring now and then so no skin forms. Cover, place in the fridge for a few hours to get really cold, then tip into an ice cream machine and freeze according to the maker's instructions. Store in the freezer until ready to use.
5 For the pears, combine the sugar with 400ml of water in a medium pan. Add the cinnamon and lemon zest, and stir over a low heat until the sugar dissolves. Carefully peel the pears, keeping the tips intact, then sit them in the liquid and cover with a cartouche (fold a square of baking paper in half three times, hold the centre point over the middle of the pan and cut in an arc along the edge to make a circle that will fit the pan). Pop the lid on and simmer for 20 minutes, until the pears are tender. Turn off the heat and let them cool in the liquid.
6 For the chocolate sauce, gently heat the cream in a pan over a medium heat until just below boiling. Remove from the heat and gradually stir in the chocolate. Whisk in about 50ml of the pear cooking liquid to loosen the sauce.
7 To serve, place a scoop of ice cream and a pear in a dish and drizzle over the sauce.
Per serving 550 cals, 32g fat (20g saturated), 4g protein, 62g carbs, 62g sugars

WHITE CHOCOLATE PANNACOTTA

Makes 6–8
- 2 gelatine leaves
- 500ml double cream
- 100ml milk
- 1 heaped tbsp sugar
- 100g white chocolate
- Fruit in syrup, to serve (optional)

1 Place the gelatine in a bowl of cold water and set aside. In a pan, heat the cream, milk and sugar until almost at boiling point. Whisk in the chocolate and gelatine, and stir until combined.
2 Pass the mixture through a sieve, and pour into moulds. Chill for at least 2–3 hours to set. Turn the pannacotta out onto plates and serve with fruit.
Per serving 487 cals, 45.5g fat (28.2g saturated), 4.7g protein, 14.9g carbs, 14.9g sugars

"Next to excellence,
 comes the appreciation of it."

William M Thackeray 1811 – 1863

Tiptree. The preserve of good taste.

Tiptree

WILKIN & SONS LIMITED TIPTREE COLCHESTER ESSEX CO5 0RF WWW.TIPTREE.COM

BAKING

Whether it's a special occasion, or simply afternoon tea time, home baking simply can't be beat. Whatever you fancy, we've got you covered, with cakes, loafs, biscuits, buns and more – we'll put the kettle on

Tiptree

SWEET POTATO, MAPLE & BACON CUPCAKES

6 Once the cakes are cold, pipe on the frosting and crumble over the bacon.

Per serving 366 cals, 18.4g fat (6.4g saturated), 3.9g protein, 62g carbs, 48.4g sugars

WINTER WONDERLAND COCONUT CAKE

Serves 20

- 375g flour
- 60g desiccated coconut
- 3 tsp baking powder
- ½ tsp salt
- 250g butter, softened
- 450g golden caster sugar
- 275ml reduced-fat coconut milk
- 3 eggs, plus 3 egg whites
- ½ tbsp vanilla extract
- Coconut or white chocolate shavings

Cream cheese icing

- 500g icing sugar
- 250g butter, softened
- 200g reduced-fat cream cheese
- 1-2 tsp coconut flavouring (or to taste), or seeds from 1 vanilla pod

1 Preheat the oven to 170C/gas 3, and grease and line 2 round 23cm cake tins. In a bowl, combine the flour, coconut, baking powder and salt.
2 In a second, large bowl, beat the butter and sugar until pale. In a jug whisk the coconut milk, whole eggs and vanilla.
3 Mix half the dry ingredients into the butter mix, followed by half the wet ingredients, and repeat until all gone.
4 Whisk the egg whites in a clean bowl to stiff peaks, then gently fold them through the mix. Divide between the 2 tins, then bake for 30–40 minutes, or until cooked. Let the cakes cool in the tins slightly, then transfer to a wire rack.
5 Meanwhile, make the icing. Using an electric mixer, beat the icing sugar and butter until smooth, then mix in the cream cheese. Stir through some coconut flavouring (or the vanilla seeds).
6 With a bread knife, slice the cakes in half through the middle. Place the bottom of 1 cake on a serving plate and spread with a thin layer of icing. Continue layering the cake and icing, finishing with icing, and decorating with shavings of coconut or white chocolate.

Per serving 501 cals, 25.7g fat (16.6g saturated), 4.7g protein, 62g carbs, 48.4g sugars

SWEET POTATO, MAPLE & BACON CUPCAKES

Makes 12

- 250g puréed cooked sweet potato
- 120ml milk
- 80ml olive oil
- 115g granulated sugar
- 100g soft light brown sugar
- 1 tsp vanilla extract
- 110g plain flour
- ½ tsp baking powder
- ½ tsp bicarbonate of soda
- 1 tsp ground cinnamon
- ½ tsp mixed spice
- 50g ground almonds

Maple frosting

- 100g unsalted butter, softened
- 225g icing sugar
- 2 tbsp maple syrup

Candied bacon

- 12 slices of rindless, thinly sliced streaky bacon or pancetta
- Maple syrup, for drizzling

1 Preheat the oven to 180C/gas 4, and line a muffin tin with cupcake cases or squares of baking paper (see picture). In a bowl, whisk the sweet potato, milk, oil, both sugars and vanilla until combined.
2 Sift the flour into a separate bowl along with the baking powder, bicarbonate of soda, spices and a pinch of salt, then stir through the ground almonds. Add to the sweet potato purée and mix until thoroughly combined.
3 Spoon the mixture into the cases, so they're two-thirds full. Bake for 20-25 minutes, until cooked through (when an inserted skewer comes out clean). Transfer to a wire rack and leave to cool.
4 For the maple frosting, beat the butter until pale, then add the icing sugar until you have a fluffy buttercream. Stir through the maple syrup, then set aside.
5 For the candied bacon, fry the bacon until crisp, then drizzle maple syrup over each piece. Transfer to a parchment lined baking tray to cool and crisp up.

Shake up your ideas of flavour combinations. On the subtle side, coconut and cream cheese bring an edge to white chocolate, while tea adds interesting essence to sponge. Go bolder by mixing savoury and sweet – sea salt gives amazing depth to milk chocolate or caramel, while vegetables like pumpkin, courgette and sweet potato add wonderfully complementary flavour and texture to cakes

SOAKED PISTACHIO & CITRUS CAKE

SOAKED PISTACHIO & CITRUS CAKE

Serves 10

- 75g unsalted butter, melted, plus extra for greasing
- 4 large eggs, separated
- 100g sugar
- 100g ground pistachios
- 100g fine semolina
- Zest of 1 lemon
- 50g no-peel orange marmalade
- 1 tsp dried mint
- 25g pistachios, finely chopped
- Greek yoghurt, to serve (optional)

Lemon syrup

- Juice of 2 lemons
- 150g sugar

1 Preheat the oven to 180C/gas 4. Grease and line a 20cm tin. Beat the egg yolks with the sugar in a mixer until creamy. While the machine is running, add the pistachios and semolina, then the butter, zest, marmalade and a pinch of salt. Beat until smooth.
2 In a separate bowl, whisk the egg whites until they form stiff peaks. Gently fold this into the pistachio mixture in three additions. Pour the batter into the prepared tin and bake for 25–30 minutes, until an inserted skewer comes out clean.
3 Make the lemon syrup. Combine the lemon juice and sugar in a saucepan and stir over a medium heat.
4 Pierce the cake all over with a skewer. Slowly pour the syrup over the cake while still warm. Sprinkle with the dried mint and pistachios. Leave the cake to cool before removing from the tin. Serve slices with Greek yoghurt, if you like.

Per serving 300 cals, 14g fat (5g saturated), 6g protein, 38g carbs, 30g sugars

MINCE PIES

Makes 16–20

- 1 tsp butter, softened, for greasing
- 1 x 411g jar good-quality mincemeat
- 2 pieces of stem ginger, chopped
- 100g hazelnuts or almonds, chopped
- 50g dried cranberries, chopped
- 50g dark chocolate, chopped (optional)
- Grated zest of 1 orange
- Grated nutmeg
- Brandy or sherry (optional)

MINCE PIES

Shortcrust pastry

- 500g plain flour, plus extra for dusting
- 100g icing sugar, plus extra for dusting
- 250g cold butter, cut into small cubes
- Finely grated zest of 1 lemon
- 2 large eggs, beaten, plus 1 for eggwash
- 1 tbsp milk

1 First, make the pastry. Sift the flour from a height into a mixing bowl, then sift in the icing sugar. Rub in the cubed butter with your fingers until crumbly, then mix in the lemon zest.
2 Add the eggs and a splash of milk and gently work everything into a smooth dough. Don't overmix, or the pastry will be chewy. On a lightly floured work surface, pat the dough into a flat round, flour it lightly, wrap in clingfilm and leave in the fridge for at least half an hour.
3 Preheat the oven to 180C/gas 4, and butter your tart tins. On a lightly floured

work surface, roll out the pastry to about 3mm thick. Cut out circles, using an 8cm pastry cutter, and press lightly in the tray holes. Chill for half an hour, setting aside the leftover pastry.
4 In a bowl, stir the mincemeat, then mix in the ginger, nuts, cranberries and chocolate (if using). Add the zest and nutmeg, a splash of brandy, and mix well.
5 Roll out the remaining pastry, then cut out circles using a 6cm pastry cutter for your pie lids. You could also cut them into stars too if you fancy it.
6 Beat 1 egg and 1 tablespoon of milk together to make an eggwash and set aside. Spoon the mincemeat into the cases to just over half full, then brush the edges with the eggwash. Lay the lids on top, press down, and brush with eggwash. Bake for 25 minutes, until the pastry is golden. Transfer to a wire rack, dust with icing sugar and serve warm.

Per serving 425 cals, 21.1g fat (10.4g saturated), 6.2g protein, 51.3 g carbs, 26g sugars

BANANA & PECAN LOAF

- 275g butter, at room temperature, plus 1 knob and extra for greasing
- 275g light brown sugar
- 3 eggs
- 100g ground almonds
- 175g self-raising flour
- 2 tbsp cocoa powder
- 1 tsp baking powder
- 150ml milk
- White chocolate, to serve

Chai buttercream filling

- 1 tbsp cardamom pods
- 5 chai tea bags
- A pinch of cracked black pepper
- 100g light brown sugar
- 100g butter, at room temperature
- 200g icing sugar
- 100g cream cheese

1 First make a chai syrup. Crack 4 of the cardamom pods and pop them in a pan with the chai tea and black pepper. Add water to cover, bring to the boil, simmer for 4 minutes, then strain. Pour the liquid back into the pan with the light brown sugar. Bring to the boil, then simmer until you have a thick syrup. Set aside.
2 Grease and line two 20cm cake tins. Preheat your oven to 180C/gas 4. Grind your remaining cardamom pods into a fine powder and set aside. Melt half the chocolate in the microwave for a few seconds. Set this aside as well.
3 Cream together 275g of butter and sugar in a bowl. Beat in the eggs one at a time, stir in the almonds, then fold through the flour, cocoa, baking powder, cardamom and ½ teaspoon of fine salt. Stir in the milk and melted chocolate.
4 Divide the mix between the tins and bake in the oven for 25–30 minutes, until an inserted skewer comes out clean. Leave in the tins for 5 minutes, before taking out to cool on a wire rack.
5 Finish the filling by beating together the butter and icing sugar with 2 tablespoons of the chai syrup until smooth. Stir in the cream cheese.
6 For the topping, melt the remaining chocolate plus a knob of butter in a bowl over a pan of simmering water, until silky.
7 To assemble, place one cake on a plate and spread with the buttercream. Top with the second cake and finish with the chocolate glaze and shavings.

Per serving 675 cals, 42.6g fat (23.6g saturated), 8.1g protein, 64g carbs, 52.7g sugars

BANANA & PECAN LOAF

Serves 12

- 110g butter, softened
- 250g light brown sugar
- 2 eggs
- 2 tbsp spiced dark rum
- 4 ripe bananas, mashed well
- 100ml buttermilk
- 270g flour
- 1 tsp baking soda
- 100g milk chocolate, roughly chopped
- 125g pecans, chopped
- A few banana chips

Pecan brittle

- 25g pecans
- 100g sugar
- ½ tsp vanilla bean paste

1 Preheat oven to 170C/gas 3. Grease and line a 25cm x 12cm loaf tin.
2 In a large bowl, cream the butter and sugar. In another bowl, lightly beat the eggs with the rum. Gradually mix the egg mixture into the butter mix, then stir in the bananas and buttermilk.
3 Sieve the flour, baking soda and a pinch of salt into a bowl, then fold into the wet mix with the chocolate and pecans. Pour into the tin and bake for 1¼ hours, or until a skewer comes out clean.
4 For the brittle, scatter the pecans on a lined baking tray. Place the sugar and vanilla bean paste in a saucepan over a low heat. Melt until golden brown, then pour over the pecans and allow to cool.
5 When the loaf is ready, let it cool in the tin. Bash the brittle into pieces. Transfer the loaf to a wire rack, and sprinkle over the brittle and banana chips.

Per serving 453 cals, 20.4g fat (7.4g saturated), 6.5g protein, 6.5g carbs, 57.6g sugars

CHOCOLATE CHAI SANDWICH CAKE

Serves 12

- 200g dark 70%-cocoa chocolate

BLUEBERRY & COCONUT CAKE

BLUEBERRY & COCONUT CAKE

Makes 9 squares

- 180g unsalted butter, softened
- 180g golden caster sugar
- 3 large eggs
- 100g flour
- 2 tsp baking powder
- 80g desiccated coconut
- 150g blueberries
- Zest and juice of 1 lime

1 Preheat the oven to 180C/gas 4. Grease and line a 20cm square cake tin. In a bowl, beat the butter and sugar until well combined. Beat in the eggs one by one, then add the flour, baking powder and coconut. Beat until smooth, then fold in the blueberries, zest and juice.
2 Bake for 35-45 minutes, until a skewer inserted into the centre comes out clean. Cool for 10 minutes, then transfer to a wire rack. Once cool, cut into squares.

Per serving 361 cals, 24.4g fat (15.1g saturated), 4.2g protein, 33.1g carbs, 23.6g sugars

DARK CHOCOLATE RICCIARELLI

Makes 25 biscuits

- 150g blanched almonds
- 200g icing sugar, plus 250g for rolling, and extra for dusting
- 2 tbsp cocoa powder
- 2 egg whites
- Seeds of 1 vanilla pod
- 1 tsp almond extract
- 100g dark chocolate, melted and cooled slightly

1 Start your biscuits the night before. Preheat the oven to 100C/gas ¼. Arrange the almonds on a baking tray and toast in the oven for 5 minutes. Remove from oven and leave to cool.
2 Put the nuts into a food processor with 2 tablespoons of the icing sugar and whizz until the texture of semolina. Sieve the rest of the icing sugar and the cocoa into a bowl, then stir in the ground almonds. Set aside.
3 In a separate bowl, whisk the egg whites to stiff peaks, then beat in the vanilla seeds and almond extract.
4 Gently fold the egg whites into the almond mix, then stir in the melted chocolate. Cover with cling film and chill in the fridge overnight.
5 The next day, preheat the oven to 160C/gas 2½. Line 2 baking trays with baking paper. Take the dough out of the fridge and leave at room temperature for 10 minutes. Dust the work surface with icing sugar, then roll the dough into a sausage. Cut it into around 25 pieces and shape into 4cm-wide balls.
6 Scatter 250g of icing sugar onto a plate. Take each ball and roll in the sugar, coating in a thick layer. Put them on the baking trays, squashing each one very lightly, so it's 1cm thick.
7 Bake the biscuits in the oven for 18-20 minutes, until crinkled on the surface. Leave to cool and firm on the trays, then transfer to a wire rack to cool completely.

Per serving 157 cals, 23.9g sugars, 5.1g fat (1.4g saturated), 2.5g protein, 24.6g carbs

DARK CHOCOLATE RICCIARELLI

Creative cakes

You can transform a sponge to suit any season by playing around with different ingredients, flavours and textures. Baking is a science but an easy way to experiment is to switch up existing ingredients. Swap your fruit - try substituting blueberries for raspberries; add lime or orange zest and juice in place of lemon; or even make a simple citrus syrup and pour over your sponge for a drizzle cake effect. If fruit isn't your thing or you want something a little richer, try adding milk, white or dark chocolate chips to your mixture; drop in a splash of almond essence; or make a simple ganache by melting cream and chocolate together then drizzle it over the top of your sponge. If you really don't want to mess with the recipe, then why not experiment with icings and buttercream.

GARLIC & ROSEMARY FOCACCIA

ALFAJORES
Makes 30 biscuits (15 sandwiches)

ALFAJORES
Makes 30 biscuits (15 sandwiches)

- 125g cornflour
- 125g self-raising flour
- 1 tsp baking powder
- ½ tsp bicarbonate of soda
- 50-75g soft unsalted butter
- 70g icing sugar
- 1 egg yolk
- 1 shot of pisco (or rum or brandy)
- ½ tsp vanilla extract

Filling
- ¼ tsp ground cinnamon
- 300g dulce de leche
- Icing sugar for dusting
- 20g desiccated coconut

1 Sift the cornflour and flour into a large bowl, add a generous pinch of sea salt, the baking powder and bicarbonate of soda, and mix together.
2 In a separate bowl, beat the butter and 50g of the icing sugar until smooth, then beat in the egg yolk, pisco and vanilla.
3 Scrape down the sides of the bowl and fold in the flour mixture until just combined - try not to overwork it.
4 Spoon the mixture onto a large piece of clingfilm, split into 2 balls and flatten into discs. Wrap in cling film and firm in the fridge for at least 1 hour.
5 Preheat the oven to 160C/gas 2-3 and line a couple of baking trays with greaseproof paper. Place each dough disc between 2 sheets of greaseproof paper and roll out to the thickness of pound coins. Use a 4cm cutter to cut out 30 biscuits, pushing the dough back together and re-rolling as needed. Transfer the biscuits to the lined trays, leaving at least 2cm between them. Place the baking trays in the fridge for 20 minutes to firm up.
6 Bake, in batches, on the middle shelf for 15-20 minutes, or until pale on top and golden underneath. Transfer to a wire rack, while you bake the next batch.
7 Mix the ground cinnamon and a good pinch of sea salt into the dulce de leche, and beat until combined. Turn over half the cooled biscuits and cover with the dulce de leche mixture, then sandwich with another biscuit. Dust the biscuits with the remaining icing sugar, then roll the edges in the desiccated coconut.

Per serving 181 cals, 4.9g fat (3.1g saturated), 1.6g protein, 31.8g carbs, 17.2g sugars

GARLIC & ROSEMARY FOCACCIA
Makes 1 loaf

- 400g strong white bread flour, plus extra for dusting
- 100g fine ground semolina flour
- 1 x 7g sachet dried yeast
- ½ tbsp sugar
- Extra virgin olive oil
- A few sprigs of fresh rosemary
- 1 garlic bulb, white skin removed

1 Put both flours and half a tablespoon of sea salt into a large mixing bowl, making a well in the middle.
2 Add 300ml lukewarm water to a measuring jug, then add the yeast and sugar and mix well. When it starts to foam, slowly pour it into the well, stirring until all the ingredients come together.
3 Dust a clean work surface with flour and knead for 5 minutes, until you get a soft, springy dough. Lightly oil a large, clean mixing bowl with some olive oil and add the dough. Dust with a little extra flour, cover with a clean tea towel and leave to prove in a warm place until doubled in size.
4 Preheat the oven to 220C/gas 7. Break apart the garlic bulb and crush the cloves, then pick the rosemary leaves. Add both to a bowl, drizzle with olive oil, season, and mix it all together.
5 Once the dough has risen, pound with your fists, then place on a baking tray (about 20cm x 30cm) and spread it out to fit. Make wells in the dough, then scatter over the garlic and rosemary, pushing them into the dips.
6 Finish with a little olive oil and sea salt. Cover with a clean tea towel and leave to rise for 20 more minutes.
7 Place the bread in the hot oven and bake for 20 minutes, or until golden on top and soft in the middle. Use a bread knife to cut it into chunks, then tuck in.

Per serving 152 cals, 0.7g fat (0.1g saturated), 5.7g protein, 30g carbs, 1.1g sugars

WALNUT BREAD

Cinnamon filling
- 100g pecans
- 75g very soft unsalted butter
- 100g dark brown sugar
- ½ tsp ground cinnamon
- 1 tsp cornflour

1 Preheat the oven to 180C/gas 4. Grease and line a 23cm springform tin. Start by preparing your filling. Place the pecans on a tray and toast in the oven for 10 minutes, then remove and leave to one side to cool completely. Finely chop the cooled nuts and set aside.
2 Meanwhile, mix the flour with 1 teaspoon of salt in a large mixing bowl, stirring to combine. Make a well in the centre and tip in the yeast. Combine the milk and butter in a small saucepan over a low heat, gently stirring until the butter has melted and the mixture is lukewarm. Pour into the flour mixture, add the egg and stir until it comes together into a soft dough.
3 Tip the dough onto a lightly floured work surface and knead well for 5 minutes. Place the dough in an oiled bowl and leave it to rise, covered with a damp tea towel, for 1 hour or until doubled in size. Tip the dough onto a lightly floured work surface and roll it out into a rectangle about 30 x 20cm.
4 To start your filling, spread the softened butter over the dough. In a bowl, mix the pecans with the brown sugar, cinnamon and cornflour, and sprinkle over your dough rectangle. Tightly roll the long side of the dough towards you, forming a Swiss roll. With a sharp knife slice the roll into 8 x 4cm thick round buns.
5 Place the buns, cut side up, in the greased tin, leaving about 1cm between each one. Leave to rise for about 30 minutes in a warm place.
6 When the buns are risen again, sprinkle with the cinnamon and granulated sugar, and bake for 20–25 minutes until golden-brown. Check after 15 minutes or so and cover the buns with foil if they are getting too brown. Remove from the oven and drizzle with the maple syrup while still in the tin. Serve warm.

Per serving 610 cals, 32g fat (8g saturated), 12g protein, 77g carbs, 27g sugars

WALNUT BREAD
Makes one 2lb loaf
- 500g wholemeal bread flour
- 1 tsp salt
- 1 x 7g yeast sachet
- 300ml lukewarm water
- 1 tbsp honey
- 1 tbsp walnut oil
- 150g walnuts, chopped
- 4 tbsp raisins

1 Place the flour, salt and yeast in a mixing bowl. In a jug stir together the water, honey and oil. Pour the wet ingredients over the dry ones and mix together to form a dough.
2 Tip the dough onto a floured surface and knead for 10 minutes until smooth and elastic. Pop into an oiled bowl and cover with clingfilm. Leave to rise for about 2 hours, until doubled in size.
3 Once risen, remove the dough from the bowl and knead in the walnuts and raisins. Shape into a 2lb loaf tin, cover and leave to prove for a further hour. Preheat the oven to 200C/gas 6.
4 Dust the loaf with a little flour and cut three slashes across the top. Place in the centre of the oven for 30 minutes, until golden brown and hollow-sounding when tapped on the bottom. Leave the loaf to cool, then slice.

Per serving 419 cals, 17.6g fat (13.1g saturated), 8.6g protein, 42.1g carbs, 41.9g sugars

PECAN, MAPLE & CINNAMON SWIRL BUNS
Makes 8
- 40g butter, plus extra for greasing
- 500g strong white bread flour
- 1 x 7g sachet dried yeast
- 275ml milk
- 1 egg
- 1 tbsp ground cinnamon
- 25g granulated sugar
- 100ml maple syrup

PECAN, MAPLE & CINNAMON SWIRL BUNS

Make an

AUTHENTIC
ITALIAN

meal of it

 BIRRA MORETTI

www.birramoretti.com
facebook.com/morettiuk | twitter.com/morettiuk

DRINKS

Don't save the cocktails for happy hour – our inventive drinks recipes will soon have you mixing and muddling like a pro! There are also zingy juices, refreshing coolers and thirst-quenching iced teas to try

LYCHEE, LIME &
COCONUT REFRESHER

STEAM DUNK
Serves 10

- 30ml lapsang spirit (mix equal parts tequila and lapsang souchong tea, then steep for 3 hours)
- 30ml Pimms
- 30ml orange juice
- 20ml sugar syrup (see pisco sour recipe page 160)
- A few drops of Angostura bitters
- Egg white
- Ground cinnamon and lemon zest, to garnish

1 Fill a cocktail shaker with ice, add the lapsang spirit, Pimms, orange juice, sugar syrup, bitters, and enough egg white to give it a creamy texture). Shake well, then strain into a glass. Garnish with cinnamon and a strip of lemon zest.

LYCHEE, LIME &
COCONUT REFRESHER
Serves 2

If you want to make this into more of a smoothie, just add a banana.

- 200g lychee flesh either fresh or tinned
- 400ml coconut milk
- 160ml coconut cream
- Juice of one lime
- 1 tsp coconut essence (optional)
- Extra lime for wedges, to serve

1 Blitz all of the ingredients in a blender Serve in tall glasses with some ice and garnish with lime wedges.

BLUEBERRY, BANANA
& OATS SMOOTHIE
Serves 2

- 200ml milk
- 3 tbsp oats
- 1 banana
- 150g blueberries
- 200ml Greek yoghurt
- Honey, to taste

1 Combine the milk and oats. Leave for at least 10 minutes. In a blender, blitz the banana, blueberries and yoghurt. Add the oaty milk and blitz again. Sweeten with a little honey, if needed. Serve over ice and garnish with extra blueberries.

MANGO, COCONUT
& LIME SMOOTHIE
Serves 2

- 100ml low-fat coconut milk
- 200ml yoghurt
- 1 ripe mango
- Juice of 1 lime

1 In a blender, blitz 100ml low-fat coconut milk, 200ml yoghurt, the flesh of a ripe mango and the juice of 1 lime. Pour over ice and garnish with mango.

BERRY & CHERRY
Serves 2

- 250g frozen berries and cherries, slightly defrosted
- 250g yoghurt
- 1 banana
- Honey

1 In a blender, blitz the berries and cherries with the yoghurt and banana. Sweeten with honey to taste, then blitz again. Serve over ice.

CUCUMBER MARGARITAS;
BASIL LEMONADE

CUCUMBER MARGARITAS

Serves 4

- 200g cucumber, chopped, plus 2 slices to serve
- 150ml 100% agave tequila
- 75ml Cointreau
- Juice of 2 lemons and 2 limes
- 75ml sugar syrup (see pisco sour recipe page 160)
- A handful of ice, plus extra to serve
- 1 tbsp sea salt

1 Place the cucumber, tequila, Cointreau, citrus juices, sugar syrup and ice into a blender and blitz well until all combined.
2 Put some crushed ice into 4 glasses and pour over the margarita. Halve the cucumber slices, coat with the sea salt and place them on the rims of the glasses. Serve immediately.

BASIL LEMONADE

Makes about 1 litre of cordial

- 450g sugar
- 6 unwaxed lemons
- A large bunch of basil, leaves picked, reserving a few for garnish
- Ice, sparkling water and 1 sliced lime, to serve

1 Gently heat 800ml water in a pan over a medium heat. Add 400g of the sugar and the finely grated zest of 4 of the lemons, stirring until the sugar has dissolved. Set aside to cool.
2 Blitz the basil in a food processor with the remaining sugar, then stir it into the sugar syrup along with the juice of all of the lemons. Leave for about 5 minutes to macerate, then strain.
3 Now you have your cordial – keep this in an airtight bottle until ready to use. To serve, pour a couple of inches into a jug or glasses over some ice, top up with sparkling water and add some lime slices.

CHILLI MOJITO-STYLE COCKTAILS

Serves 6

- 1 heaped tbsp brown sugar
- 1 bunch of mint, leaves picked
- 1 red chilli, halved lengthways
- Juice of 4 limes
- 200ml gin
- 2 large handfuls of ice
- 1.5 litres tonic water
- 1 egg white
- 1 tsp red chilli flakes
- 1 heaped tbsp sugar

1 Place the brown sugar, mint, fresh chilli and lime juice in a large jug. Muddle with a wooden spoon, mixing it all together to get the flavours going. Add the gin and ice and top up with the tonic water.

2 Lightly whisk the egg white in a large bowl and in a second bowl mix the chilli flakes and sugar. Dip the rims of the glasses in the egg white, then in the sugar and chilli mixture, twisting it around to coat the rims of the glasses. Discard the halved chilli, pour and serve.

BLACKCURRANT & ELDERFLOWER SPRITZER

Serves 2

- A handful of blackcurrants
- A few sprigs of rosemary
- 50ml elderflower cordial
- 150ml white wine
- A little soda water

1 Add a handful of blackcurrants and fresh rosemary to a large jug or jar and crush everything together with a spoon. Add the elderflower cordial and leave to infuse for 30 minutes – or as long as possible. To serve, throw in a handful of ice cubes, the white wine and top up with soda water.

NEW BLOSSOM

TIKI MIKI

NEW BLOSSOM
Serves 1
- Juice and zest of 1 lemon
- 60ml cachaça
- 20ml sugar syrup (see pisco sour recipe, far right)
- 2 drops orange blossom water
- Pulp of 1 passion fruit
- Good-quality lemonade
- Mint sprigs, to garnish

1 Mix everything except the lemonade and mint in a glass. Add ice, top up with lemonade and garnish with mint. (Or up the quantities for a party punch.)

TIKI MIKI
Serves 1
- 60ml Ron Zacapa 23 golden rum
- 40ml each of orange & pineapple juice
- 30ml apple syrup
- 10ml absinthe
- Pineapple, to garnish

1 Shake the rum, juices, apple syrup and absinthe in a cocktail shaker. Serve in a chilled glass with a slice of pineapple.

SALLY COME BACK
Serves 1
- 60ml gold tequila
- 60ml cranberry juice
- 20ml lemon juice
- 20ml grenadine syrup
- 20ml acerola or cherry liqueur

1 Fill a cocktail shaker with ice. Add all the ingredients and shake well. Strain into a chilled cocktail glass without ice.

RHUBARB & BASIL SMOOTHIE
Serves 2
- 300g rhubarb, chopped
- A small bunch of basil
- 3 tbsp agave nectar
- 150ml apple juice
- 250g low-fat yoghurt

1 Cook the rhubarb, agave and a splash of water over a medium heat for 8-10 minutes, until soft. In a blender, blitz with remaining ingredients until smooth.

BLACKBERRY BELLINI
Serves 6
- 200g blackberries
- 2 tbsp sugar
- 1 bottle of prosecco or champagne

1 Preheat your oven to 200C/gas 6. Tip the blackberries into a roasting dish and scatter over the sugar. Roast for 10 minutes. Remove and leave to cool.

2 In a blender, blitz the berries to a purée, pass through a sieve, then chill. 3 Evenly distribute the chilled fruit among 6 champagne glasses and top up with your favourite bubbles.

PISCO SOUR
For a sugar syrup bring 200g sugar and 200ml water to the boil. Simmer until dissolved and the liquid is clear.
Serves 1
- 60ml pisco
- 30ml sugar syrup
- 30ml lime or lemon juice
- ½ egg white
- Angostura bitters

1 Fill a cocktail shaker with ice and add the pisco, sugar syrup, juice and egg white. Shake, then pour into a chilled glass with 2 drops of Angostura bitters.

ORANGE, CARROT, APPLE & GINGER JUICE
Serves 2
- 2 apples
- 2 carrots
- 1-2 oranges
- 2cm piece of ginger, peeled

1 Juice everything, adding a splash of water if you like, and serve.

BAKED BLACKBERRY BELLINIS

PINEAPPLE, ORANGE, PASSION
FRUIT & MINT SMOOTHIE

PINEAPPLE, ORANGE, PASSION FRUIT & MINT SMOOTHIE

Serves 2

- 200g chopped pineapple
- 1 tbsp honey
- Juice of 3 large oranges
- Mint leaves
- 2 Passion fruits

1 In a blender, purée the pineapple and honey. Add a quarter of the orange juice, a few mint leaves, then blitz again.
2 Scoop the flesh from the passion fruits into a bowl and stir to loosen the pulp. Add to the jug (strain first if you like) with the remaining orange. Stir and serve over ice.

AYRAN

Serves 2

A great cooler, served with spicy dishes.

- 300ml plain yoghurt
- 200ml sparkling water
- Chopped mint and ground coriander, to serve

1 Whisk together the yoghurt, sparkling water and ½ teaspoon of salt. Pour into glasses, then sprinkle with the chopped mint ground and coriander, to serve.

CUCUMBER, LEMONGRASS & LIME AGUA FRESCA

Makes 1 jug

- 175g sugar
- 4 cucumbers, roughly chopped
- 2 lemongrass stalks, roughly chopped
- 4 juicy limes
- Ice and fresh mint, to serve

1 In a medium saucepan, heat together the sugar and 500ml water, stirring, until the sugar has dissolved. Set aside to cool. Meanwhile, whizz the cucumber and lemongrass in a food processor until everything is well combined, then squeeze in the juice from the limes. Pass through a fine sieve into a jug, then add the sugar syrup. Stir well to combine, then divide among glasses and serve with plenty of ice and a sprig of mint.

ICED MINT TEA WITH HONEY & ROSEWATER

Serves 2

- 1 bunch of mint
- 1½ tbsp runny honey
- A few drops of rosewater
- Cucumber, to garnish

1 Steep the mint and runny honey in a teapot of hot water for 10 minutes. Strain into a jug and leave to cool completely. Pour into glasses over ice, and add a few drops of rose water and some cucumber slices, to garnish.

LOBSTER CAESAR COCKTAILS

CHRISTMAS PUDDING VODKA

LOBSTER CAESAR COCKTAILS

Upgrade a classic with the addition of lobster claws - it'll definitely impress!

Serves 2

- Celery salt
- 1 lemon, ½ cut into 2 wedges and ½ sliced
- 4 shots of vodka
- Tabasco sauce
- Worcestershire sauce
- 1 tsp horseradish sauce
- Clamato juice (see note)
- 2 large cooked lobster or crab claws, cracked
- 2 celery sticks, leaves on

1 Sprinkle a saucer generously with celery salt. Take two large glasses and run a lemon wedge around the rim of each one, then dip in the celery salt, shaking off any excess.
2 Fill the glasses with ice and add 2 shots of vodka to each glass. Add the tabasco, Worcestershire and horseradish sauce, to taste.
3 Give the cocktails a good stir and top up each glass with clamato juice. Pop a lobster or crab claw and celery stalk into each cocktail, garnish with a slice of lemon and serve.
Note Clamato juice is a savoury tomato and clam juice that's perfect for cocktails. Available at melburyandappleton.co.uk.

CHRISTMAS PUDDING VODKA

Makes 1-1.5 litres

- 1 blade of mace
- 2 cinnamon sticks
- 450g light muscovado sugar
- 300g currants
- 200g chopped mixed peel
- 2 tbsp freshly squeezed orange juice
- 2 tbsp freshly squeezed lemon juice
- Grated rind of 1 lemon
- Grated rind of 1 orange
- 2 tsp ground mixed spice
- 1 litre good quality vodka

1 Warm the spices in a dry pan over a low heat for 10 minutes until fragrant.
2 Add to a bowl with all the remaining ingredients, mix, cover and chill for 3-4 days, stirring a few times daily.
3 To bottle the vodka, line a sieve with muslin and strain. Discard the cinnamon sticks but reserve the soaked fruits for other uses. Decant the vodka into clean bottles and seal. This will store for up to one year in a cool dark place.

KION

Serves 1

- 60ml pisco
- 30ml lemon juice
- 20ml sugar syrup (see pisco sour recipe on previous spread)

- A few thin matchsticks of ginger
- ½ egg white
- 1 tbsp passion fruit and orange jam (mix 40g orange marmalade with the pulp of 1 passion fruit - keep any left over for next time!)
- Mint, to garnish

1 Fill a cocktail shaker with ice. Add the pisco, lemon juice, sugar syrup, ginger and egg white. Shake really well, then pour into a tall chilled glass and add the passion fruit and orange jam. Garnish with a sprig of mint.

FRANGELICO & BRANDY HOT CHOCOLATE

Serves 8

- 500ml whole milk
- 500ml semi-skmmed milk
- 200ml Frangelico
- 200ml brandy
- 140g good-quality chocolate, grated
- 2 tbsp cocoa powder
- Sugar, to taste

1 Heat the whole milk until boiling. Stir in the semi-skimmed milk, Frangelico, brandy, grated chocolate and cocoa powder, then whisk together until all the chocolate has melted. Add a little sugar to taste and serve immediately.

Match point!

Matching food and wine has become second nature. We might like Chablis or Sancerre with our sea bass or a Bordeaux with our beef – but how many of us would consider a fine Italian lager with our risotto?

And yet, while the liquid may be different, the principles are the same: the flavours and acidity in the beer give clues as to what food will provide its perfect foil. Indeed, certain beers, like certain wines, possess particularly strong food-friendly credentials. Step forward Birra Moretti, the expression of an authentic Italian brewing tradition dating back more than 150 years.

Since 1859, when Luigi Moretti founded his "Beer & Ice Factory" in the north-eastern town of Udine, Birra Moretti has been made using only the finest ingredients, particularly a special type of hop that provides its unique aroma and enhances its perfectly poised bitterness. Straw-yellow, delicately malty and bottom-fermented to a strength of 4.6%, it has the balance to complement a broad range of foods.

NEGRONI SPARKLERS

NEGRONI SPARKLERS
Serves 10
- Zest and juice of 2 oranges
- 4 tbsp smooth orange marmalade
- 250ml Campari
- 1 bottle of prosecco, chilled

1 Pop the orange zest and juice and the marmalade in a small pan over a low heat. Stir everything together, then simmer for 5 minutes until it forms a smooth syrup. Set aside to cool.
2 In a jug, mix the cooled syrup with the Campari, then pour a little into the bottom of the champagne saucers. Top up each one with chilled prosecco and garnish with a sliver of orange peel.

DARK BERRY & ROSEMARY-JUNIPER GIN FIZZ
There's something satisfyingly British about this hedgerow mojito. Its zippy juniper-herbaceous edge is a welcome change from rich festive drinks. You could also use raspberries if you like.
Serves 10
- 500g frozen blackberries
- 4 lemons, chopped into little pieces
- 2 sprigs of rosemary, leaves picked
- 10 juniper berries
- 5 tbsp honey
- 500ml good quality gin
- 1 litre soda water

1 Divide the blackberries, lemons and rosemary evenly between each tumbler, then add a juniper berry and ½ tbsp honey. These can be made ahead of time and can sit in the fridge until your guests arrive.
2 When you're ready to serve, use a muddler or rolling pin to mash the berry mixture until the fruit is crushed. Fill each glass with ice, top with 50ml gin and a dash of soda water, stir well and serve. Garnish with extra frozen blackberries.

DARK BERRY & ROSEMARY-JUNIPER GIN FIZZ

This versatility lends itself in particular to the less formal atmosphere of the gastropub, where great food, unfussily prepared and presented, is the order of the day. In particular, just as wines can find their best expression alongside the foods of their own region, so Moretti is most at home with Italian dishes.

Risottos, pasta, main courses involving white meat, delicately flavoured cheeses – discovering your favourite gastropub food match for Birra Moretti is a fascinating and tasty voyage of discovery. It's a thoroughly modern way of getting to know a beer whose fame has spread far beyond its homeland's borders, to the 40-plus countries all over the world where it is now exported.

But, while Birra Moretti has found fame and fortune since its creation, it has also stayed true to its own tradition – still brewed to traditional methods, using superior ingredients and a blend of high-quality hops and malts. In essence, an embodiment of Italian craftsmanship and passion for quality. *For more information, log on to birramoretti.com.*

Steak+k

Delicious, pure and versatile

Kikkoman's natural ingredients and traditional brewing methods make a unique soy seasoning that brings out the best flavours in just about everything. Splash, dash or brush; adding such a pure seasoning to your cooking is so simple.

SAUCES & EXTRAS

Don't underestimate the importance of a good sauce, gravy or chutney – they can completely transform a meal. Make batches ahead and store in the fridge or freezer to ensure your food is never short of a good complement

kikkoman®
seasoning your life

MANGO CHUTNEY

Infused oils

Chutneys are a great way of preserving fruit and veg. Balancing the sugar and vinegar element is the key and adding aromats and spice gives depth of flavour. Apples, tomatoes and onions pair beautifully with cinnamon, ginger and allspice. Plums and figs work well with shallots, ginger, orange and cloves. But it's not just about fruit, vegetables work too. Runner beans with mustard and coriander seeds and a hit of chilli are delicious. A good place to start is a basic red onion chutney – great with warm goats cheese, a classic Christmas cheese board, or simply dolloped in a sarnie. Soften your onions in a pan with some oil, add a splash of red wine and balsamic vinegar, balance with demerara sugar to taste and cook down. Store in sterilised jars, ready for eating.

1 Heat a frying pan over a medium heat. Add the hazelnuts and lightly toast, shaking the pan to stop them burning. Use a pestle and mortar to smash up roughly, then transfer the nuts to a dish. Toast the sesame, coriander and cumin seeds in the frying pan, being careful not to burn them. Use the pestle and mortar to grind them together with the peppercorns. Add the crushed hazelnuts, paprika and salt, then mix it all together. Store the dukkah in an airtight container.

MANGO CHUTNEY
Makes about 800ml
- 2kg firm but ripe mangoes
- 500ml white wine vinegar
- 400g granulated sugar
- 1 tsp cumin seeds
- 1 tsp coriander seeds
- Seeds of 8 cardamom pods
- 1 tsp chilli powder
- 2 tsp nigella seeds
- 2 tsp salt
- A large thumb-sized piece of ginger
- 2 cloves garlic, chopped
- 1 red chilli, finely chopped

1 Peel, stone and roughly chop the mangoes; set aside. Add the vinegar and sugar to a pan over a medium heat, stirring until the sugar dissolves. Bring to the boil and reduce by a few centimetres.
2 Meanwhile, gently toast the cumin, coriander and cardamom seeds until aromatic. Add to a mortar with the chilli powder and crush with the pestle into

a fine powder. Add this to the vinegar pan, along with the mango, nigella seeds and salt. Grate in the ginger, add the garlic and bring everything to a boil. Simmer for 45 minutes until the mixture has a thick, syrupy consistency.
3 Add the chopped chilli for the last 10 minutes. Divide among sterilised jars, seal and keep for up to 6 months.

DUKKAH
This Egyptian medley of nuts and spices is lovely sprinkled over veg or fish, or served as a dip with bread, alongside a good olive oil.
Makes 80-100g
- 40g whole hazelnuts
- 25g sesame seeds
- 3 tsp coriander seeds
- 1½ tsp cumin seeds
- 1 tsp peppercorns
- ½ tsp paprika
- 1 tsp sea salt

ASIAN PICKLED ROOT VEG
Makes 1 x 500g jar
- 150ml rice wine vinegar
- 1 red chilli, sliced
- 2 tbsp sugar
- 1-2 handfuls of finely sliced carrots, turnips and radishes
- Coriander and mint

1 Heat the rice wine vinegar in a pan with the red chilli and sugar, stirring until the sugar dissolves. Pop the veg in a large bowl and pour over the pickling liquid. Leave to cool. Add the coriander and mint, spoon into a jar and seal. Store in the fridge and eat within 1 month.

MIXED HERBS BUTTER

BASIL, GARLIC & CHILLI VINEGAR

MIXED HERBS BUTTER

Makes about 150g

- 150g softened butter
- 1 tbsp each of chopped parsley, dill, chives and basil
- 1 garlic clove, crushed
- Juice of ½ lemon

1 In a small bowl combine the softened butter and the chopped herbs. Stir in the garlic and lemon juice. Mix well to combine and serve with grilled corn on the cob.

BASIL, GARLIC & CHILLI VINEGAR

Makes about 500ml

- 4 garlic cloves, squashed
- 10g basil leaves, torn
- 2 red chillies, halved and deseeded
- 500ml cider vinegar

1 Put the garlic, basil, chillies and cider vinegar in a pan. Bring to the boil and simmer for about 5 minutes.
2 Cool, strain, return garlic and chilli to vinegar, then store in a sterilised bottle.

STICKY ONION GRAVY

Serves 4

- 20g butter
- 2-3 onions, finely sliced

- 2 garlic cloves, finely chopped
- 2 tsp flour
- ½ glass of red wine
- 250ml chicken or vegetable stock
- 1-2 tbsp balsamic vinegar

1 Melt the butter in a shallow pan over a medium heat. Add the onion and garlic, then cook until golden and soft. Add a splash of water any time it looks too dry.
2 Cook, lid on, for another 10 minutes over a low heat. The onions should be falling apart and a deep brown colour.
3 Stir in the flour and cook for a couple of minutes. Add the red wine, reduce and cook off the alcohol for about 2-5 minutes, then add the stock. Season.
4 Stir for 15 minutes more, or until the gravy is soft and sticky, stirring through a splash of balsamic vinegar.

BLUEBERRY SAUCE

Makes about 400ml

- 400g fresh or frozen blueberries
- Juice of 1 orange
- 30g golden caster sugar
- 1 tbsp cornflour (optional)

1 In a small pan cook the blueberries, orange juice and sugar over a low heat until the mixture is soft and sticky. If you would prefer a thicker sauce, stir in 1 tbsp cornflour. Cook for 2 more minutes.

SEA SALT CARAMEL PORK CRACKLING

Serves 8-10

- 750g pork rind, scored (ask your butcher to do this for you)
- 1 tsp chilli flakes
- 1 tsp fennel seeds
- 2 tbsp sea salt
- Olive oil
- 100g golden caster sugar

1 If you have enough time, dry out the pork rind for 24 hours beforehand, by leaving it laid out on a tray in the fridge.
2 Using a pestle and mortar, bash the chilli, fennel seeds and sea salt until you have a fine powder.
3 Slice the rind into large strips and massage in the chilli mix, rubbing in a little olive oil. Leave to marinate for 1 hour. Preheat your oven to 220C/gas 7.
4 Place the rind in a baking tray and roast for around 20 minutes until golden.
5 Line a tray with greaseproof paper. When the crackling is ready, take it out of the oven, break it into bite-size pieces and spread it out on the prepared tray.
6 Place the sugar in a heavy pan with 50ml of water and gently bring it to the boil. Keep it boiling for 10 minutes, until the mixture is golden and caramelised. Drizzle it over the crackling and leave to set. Once totally hardened it's ready for eating - perfect with a cold beer.

SALTED CARAMEL FUDGE

PICKLED CHILLIES

SALTED CARAMEL FUDGE

Makes 40-50 pieces

- 600g sugar
- 250ml double cream
- 50g unsalted butter

1 Melt 200g of the sugar in a pan over a medium heat until golden, then beat in the rest, along with the double cream, butter and ½-1 teaspoon of salt.
2 Stir over a medium-high heat until it reaches 118C on a sugar thermometer.
3 Off the heat, beat with an electric mixer until thick. Pour into a lined 20 x 20cm tin, leave to cool, then chill for 2-3 hours to set. Sprinkle with a pinch of sea salt, cut into 2-3cm squares and serve.

PICKLED CHILLIES

Makes 1 x 1.5 litre jar

- 20 mixed chillies, halved lengthways
- 5 peppercorns
- 3 bay leaves
- 1 tsp yellow mustard seeds
- 1 litre white wine vinegar
- A pinch of golden caster sugar

1 Put the mixed chillies, peppercorns, bay leaves and mustard seeds in a sterilised 1.5 litre jar. Add the vinegar, 500ml of water and a pinch each of salt and golden caster sugar.

2 Mix it all together and seal. Leave for a few days before eating. Once opened, the chillies will keep for 2 weeks.

PEPPERCORN SAUCE FOR STEAK

Serves 2-4

- 60ml brandy
- A knob of butter
- 75ml stock
- 1 tsp mixed peppercorns
- 80ml single cream

1 Fry your steak to your liking, then set aside. Over a medium heat, deglaze the pan with the brandy and butter. Stir in the stock and peppercorns, then simmer for 3-5 minutes.
2 Swirl in the single cream and cook, stirring, for 1-2 minutes. Remove the sauce from the heat and serve immediately with the rested steak.

BEARNAISE SAUCE

Serves 6

- 220g unsalted butter
- 1 tbsp white wine vinegar
- 2 small shallots, finely chopped
- 4 egg yolks
- 1 small bunch each of tarragon and parsley, leaves picked and chopped
- Lemon juice

1 Add the butter, white wine vinegar and shallots to a medium-sized pan and place over a medium heat. Bring to the boil, then reduce to a simmer and bubble away until reduced by half.
2 Strain the liquid into a jug and set aside. Whisk the egg yolks with a tablespoon of water in a non-stick pan over a low heat until slightly thickened. Slowly pour in the butter mixture, whisking until the sauce has thickened.
3 Season with salt and pepper, add the herbs and a squeeze or two of lemon juice to taste. Serve alongside a steak, skinny fries and a crisp green salad.

KALE CRISPS

Serves 4-6

- 2 litres vegetable oil
- 2 generous handfuls of kale, stalks removed, leaves torn into bite-size bits

1 Pour the vegetable oil into a deep pan and place over a medium heat. Wait for it to reach about 190C - you can test it by dropping a little kale into the pan; if it bubbles up, then the oil is ready.
2 Using tongs, carefully lower the kale into the hot oil and cook in batches for 5 minutes, or until crisp. Remove with a slotted spoon and drain on sheets of kitchen paper. Leave to cool and serve sprinkled with a little sea salt.

CHILLI JAM

Makes 3 x 250ml jars

- 6 red chillies, roughly chopped
- 1 small red pepper, deseeded and roughly chopped
- 500g preserving sugar
- 300ml white wine vinegar

1 Whizz the chillies and pepper in a food processor until finely chopped.
2 Put the sugar and vinegar in a saucepan over a medium heat and stir until the sugar dissolves.
3 Add the chillies and pepper, stir, then turn up the heat and bring to the boil. Let it bubble for 10 minutes, until the mixture thickens. Pour into sterilised jars and let it cool, then seal the lids.

AUBERGINE DIP

You'll need to start making this the day before you want to serve it. Don't use metal bowls or utensils, as they will turn the aubergine black.

Serves 6-8

- 4 large aubergines, very ripe and soft to the touch
- ½ lemon
- 1 garlic clove
- 2 tbsp tahini
- 500g fat-free Greek yoghurt
- 100ml olive oil
- 1 small bunch of flat leaf parsley
- Salad and flatbreads, to serve

1 Using tongs, hold the aubergines directly over the gas flame on the hob until charred. The skin will start to split and you will see steam billowing out. Take them off the heat and leave overnight in a colander to drain.
2 The following day, peel the aubergines. Put the flesh in a bowl and squeeze over the lemon juice. Squash the juice into the aubergines with a wooden spoon then leave it in the fridge for 6 hours.
3 Finely chop the aubergine on a large board, then add the finely chopped garlic and mix it in with a pinch of salt. Tip the aubergine and garlic into a bowl – wooden is best, but glass or ceramic is also fine – and, using a wooden spoon, mix in the tahini, yoghurt and olive oil until combined. Sprinkle with parsley and serve with a green salad and some toasted flatbreads.

CHILLI JAM

TZATZIKI

Strain the liquid from the cucumber to ensure that your tzatziki is lovely and creamy, not watery.

Makes 1 small bowlful

- 1 cucumber
- 100g Greek-style yoghurt
- 1 garlic clove, crushed
- 20g fresh mint leaves, finely chopped
- 1 tbsp dried mint
- Pitta, to serve

1 Using a coarse grater, grate the cucumber onto a piece of muslin or other thin, clean cloth. Sprinkle with a good pinch of salt - this will draw out the liquid from the cucumber. Leave for 5 minutes. Meanwhile, combine the yoghurt, garlic and both mints in a bowl. Scrunch the cucumber up in the muslin and hold it over the sink while twisting the top to strain any excess moisture. Mix into the yoghurt, then serve with pitta. Store in an airtight container in the fridge.

Don't let chillies go off. Allow red chillies to dry out completely, then crumble over cooked spaghetti, tossed with olive oil and chopped parsley for a simple supper. Or stir into a curry at the start of cooking to provide a smoky, background heat. Make a chilli oil by heating dried chillies in a pan, cover with olive oil, then pour into a bottle. Give it a shake every now and then. Alternatively, pop them in a plastic container in the freezer; grate your frozen chillies into your cooking

BERRY COULIS

Makes 200-250ml

- 400g fresh or frozen raspberries
- Juice of 1 lemon
- 3 tbsp icing sugar

1 In a food processor, blitz the raspberries and pass through a sieve to strain. Mix with the lemon juice and icing sugar, adding more of either until the flavours are to your liking.

4 Remove and discard the skins of the peppers and roughly chop the flesh. Using a large pestle and mortar, pound the garlic cloves with a good pinch of sea salt until the garlic begins to break down. 5 Add the toasted nuts and continue to bash until you have a coarse paste. Add the tomatoes and peppers and pound until breaking down. Add the toasted bread and paprikas and pound until the whole lot has formed a lovely coarse paste. Stir in a glug of olive oil, the vinegar and a splash of water. Season to taste, adding a little extra vinegar if you want more of a tang.

MANGO & LIME COULIS

Makes 200–250ml

- 2 ripe mangoes
- Juice and zest of 2–3 limes
- 2–3 tbsp icing sugar

1 Peel the mango and add the flesh to a food processor. Blitz with the lime juice and zest until really smooth. Stir in the icing sugar, adding it in small amounts until it's as sweet as you'd like, and blitz again well until combined. This is lovely served over fruity sorbet or ice cream.

CHERRY COMPOTE

CHERRY COMPOTE

Makes 1 x 600g jar

- 1.5kg fresh cherries, pitted
- 300g sugar
- Zest and juice of 1 orange
- 1 vanilla pod, split in half

1 Place all the ingredients in a medium-sized pan and bring to the boil. Reduce the heat to low and simmer for about 10 minutes, or until the cherries have softened and released their juices. Stir the compote and continue cooking for 45 minutes, or until thickened. Allow to cool, spoon into sterilised jars and seal.

ROMESCO SAUCE

Serves 4 as a sauce or dip

- 4 long red peppers
- 25g blanched almonds
- 25g blanched hazelnuts
- 1 slice stale good-quality bread, chopped into pieces
- Extra virgin olive oil
- 4 garlic cloves
- 2 ripe tomatoes
- 1 tsp sweet smoked paprika
- 1 tsp paprika
- 2 tbsp sherry vinegar

1 Preheat the oven to 220C/gas 7. Spread the peppers on a baking tray and roast on the top shelf of the oven for 30–40 minutes, turning, until blackened all over. Transfer to a bowl, cover with clingfilm and set aside to cool (the steam will help loosen the skins). 2 Meanwhile, toast the almonds and hazelnuts in a dry frying pan over a medium heat for 1 minute, or until they begin to darken and give off a lovely nutty aroma. Remove from the heat and set aside for later. 3 Return the pan to the heat, add the chopped bread, drizzle with olive oil and toast for 5 minutes, until lightly golden on all sides, then set aside.

SATAY SAUCE

Our version of this south-east Asian recipe uses low-fat coconut cream.

Makes 400ml

- 160ml low-fat coconut cream
- 150g dry-roasted peanuts
- 2 garlic cloves, grated
- 2 tbsp light brown sugar
- 1 tbsp dark soy sauce
- 1 tbsp sesame oil
- 1 tbsp fish sauce
- Zest and juice of 1 lime
- 2cm piece of root ginger, grated
- ½ red chilli, deseeded and finely chopped

1 Blitz all the ingredients in a food processor, then pop in a jar and refrigerate until needed. Use the satay as a dipping sauce with crunchy vegetable sticks or as a marinade for strips of chicken or beef before skewering them, then cooking on the barbecue or a griddle pan.

MANGO & LIME COULIS

ORANGE CHOCOLATE SAUCE

ORANGE CHOCOLATE SAUCE

Makes 350-400ml

- 150g dark chocolate
- 300ml whipping cream
- Zest of 1 orange

1 Gently melt the dark chocolate with the cream. Grate in the orange zest and cook gently for 1-2 minutes. Keep the sauce warm before serving or, if making ahead, gently reheat when ready to use. This is perfect drizzled over vanilla ice cream.

APPLE & TOMATO CHUTNEY

Makes 6 x 300ml jars

- 1kg russet apples, peeled, cored and chopped
- 750g granulated sugar
- 500g tomatoes, chopped
- 150g sultanas
- 1 litre malt vinegar
- 30g piece of ginger, peeled and grated
- 2 onions, sliced
- 2 cinnamon sticks
- 1 tbsp crushed allspice
- 1 tbsp mustard seeds
- 1 tbsp salt

1 In a large saucepan, slowly bring all of the ingredients to the boil. Simmer gently over a low heat for 2½-3 hours, until thickened and reduced by half.
2 Spoon into warm sterilised jars, seal and store until ready to use.

CRANBERRY RELISH

Great with a roast, or spread in a chicken and salad sandwich.

Makes 1 x 500g jars

- Peel and juice of 1 orange
- 500g frozen cranberries
- 1 piece of stem ginger, chopped
- 4 tbsp demerara sugar
- 3 cloves
- 1 cinnamon stick
- A splash of port (optional)

1 Place all of the ingredients in a pan and bring to the boil. Reduce the heat and simmer for around 30 minutes, stirring occasionally, until glossy. Remove the cloves and cinnamon stick. Leave the relish to cool and spoon into a sterilized 500g jar.

RED PEPPER PESTO

Makes enough to serve 4 with pasta

- 1 jar of roasted red peppers
- 200g parmesan, grated
- 100g pine nuts
- A bunch of thyme
- Extra virgin olive oil

1 Blitz the peppers in a food processor with the parmesan, pine nuts, thyme and enough olive oil to loosen. Drain and stir through half the pesto (save the rest). Add a little water to loosen and top with extra parmesan. Perfect mixed with pasta, such as fusilli or penne.

FIG & RED ONION CHUTNEY

Makes 2 x 500g jars

- 400g dried figs
- 1 tbsp olive oil
- 2 red onions, sliced
- 3 tbsp soft brown sugar
- 4 cloves
- 6 peppercorns
- 1 tbsp red wine vinegar
- A handful walnut halves (optional)

1 Place the figs in a bowl, pour over just enough boiling water to cover and leave to soak. Place a pan over a medium heat, add the olive oil and red onion, and cook for about 10 minutes, until soft. Sprinkle over the sugar and stir until dissolved. Drain the figs and add to the onion pan with the cloves, peppercorns, vinegar and 150ml water. Stir in the walnut halves (if using), bring to the boil, then reduce the heat and cook for a further 10 minutes. Leave to cool, then spoon into a sterilised jar.

SPECIAL OFFER

Get your regular copy of Jamie magazine & receive a free copy of Save With Jamie

If you've enjoyed these recipes, you'll be pleased to know that you can subscribe to the regular magazine for just £27.95 a year – saving 30% on the cover price. Not only that, pay by direct debit and we'll send you a free copy of *Save With Jamie*, the bestselling new cookbook from Jamie Oliver.

SAVE *with* JAMIE

SHOP SMART
COOK CLEVER
WASTE LESS

120 TASTY
MONEY
SAVING
MEALS

GREAT REASONS TO SUBSCRIBE

- Save 30% on the cover price
- Get a free copy of *Save With Jamie* (rrp £26)*
- 75+ recipes in every issue, including exclusive new recipes from Jamie Oliver

and some of the world's best chefs and food writers
- All recipes road-tested in the Jamie Oliver test kitchens, to make sure they work time after time

Call us now on
0800 953 9800
and quote code YB5

(Lines open 8am–8pm Mon-Fri; 9am–1pm Sat)

Order online at
jamiemagazine.com/YB5

YEARBOOK INDEX

Editor
Andy Harris

Managing editor
Paul Dring

Art director
Adrienne Pitts

Deputy art director
Helen Little

Sub editor
Claire Nelson

Editorial assistant
Clare Knivett

Licensing & syndication
Mandie Howard

Editor at large
Jamie Oliver

Contributors
Hanife Anur, Carolyn Barber, Michelle Berriedale-
Johnson, Chris Bianco, Alain Bosse, Tony Briscoe,
Diego Cabrera, Dario Cecchini, Charlie Clapp,
Samantha Clark, Samuel Clark, Gennaro Contaldo,
Laura Edwards, Abigail Fawcett, Tara Fisher, Laura
Fyfe, Jonathan Gregson, Andy Harris, Lizzie Harris,
Georgina Hayden, Will Heap, Joss Herd, Amanda
Heywood, Cara Hobday, Ken Hom, Anna Jones, Dan
Jones, Emma Lee, Giorgio Locatelli, David Loftus,
Christina Mackenzie, Kate McCullough, Andrew
Montgomery, Gareth Morgan, David Munns, Myles
New, Nathan Outlaw, Bianca Nice, Jamie Oliver,
Martin Poole, Con Poulos, Rebecca Rauter, Jon
Rotheram, Matt Russell, Anders Schønnemann,
Phillippa Spence, Brett Stevens, Sam Stowell,
Yuki Sugiura, Jemma Watts.
Yearbook illustration by Julia Rothman

Advertising
Rob Biagioni, John Brown Media, 020 7565 3206
rob.biagioni@johnbrownmedia.com
Gayle Curtis, John Brown Media, 020 7565 3313
gayle.curtis@johnbrownmedia.com

Jamie Oliver Ltd
CEO John Jackson
Managing director Tara Donovan
Head of legal Giovanna Milia

Subscriptions Jamie Magazine, Regal Place,
Maxwell Road, London SW6 2HD. 020 7814 5064,
jamie@subscriptions-mps.co.uk

For subscription enquiries in Australia and New Zealand,
email customercare@mymagazinesubscription.com.au or
telephone +61 1300 716 426. Postal enquiries can be
directed to Jamie Magazine, Locked Bag 527,
Frenchs Forest, NSW, 2086, Australia.

Distribution by Mail Publisher Solutions, Northcliffe House,
2 Derry Street, London W8 5TT, +44 20 3615 2790

Jamie magazine is published by Jamie Magazine Ltd. Registered
Office 19–21 Nile Street, London N1 7LL, UK; 020 3375 5101.
Jamie is a registered trademark. Copyright 2013 Jamie Magazine
Ltd. Any reproduction without permission is prohibited. Jamie
magazine contains editorial content from external contributors,
which does not necessarily reflect the views of Jamie Magazine
Ltd. Jamie magazine does not accept or respond to unsolicited
manuscripts and photographs. The publishers do not accept
responsibility for errors in advertisements or third-party offers.
Jamie magazine is printed in the UK by Southernprint Ltd. Print
management & reprographic services by John Brown.

Member of the Audit Bureau of Circulations

Useful information

Weight	
Imperial	**Metric**
1 oz	28g
1 lb	450g

Liquid	
1 teaspoon	5ml
1 dessertspoon	12ml
1 tablespoon	15ml
1 shot	25ml
1 small wine glass	125ml
1 large wine glass	250ml
1 fl oz	30ml
1 pint	568ml
1 glug	about 20ml

Cup measures		
	US	**AUS**
1 cup sugar	200g	220g
1 cup flour	115g	125g
1 cup liquid	240ml	250ml

Oven temperatures		
Celsius	**Fahrenheit**	**Gas Mark**
110C	225F	¼
130C	250F	½
140C	275F	1
150C	300F	2
170C	325F	3
180C	350F	4
190C	375F	5
200C	400F	6
220C	425F	7
230C	450F	8

For fan-assisted ovens, reduce temperatures by 10–20C

Ingredients

- We use Freedom Foods certified, free-range or organic pork and chicken and their by-products, including large eggs with an average weight of 60g.
- Whenever possible, we look for sustainably managed fish, with an MSC or Freedom Foods mark.
- We use either beef gelatine or vegetarian setting agents, such as agar agar, and adjust for liquid quantity used in recipe according to packet instructions.
- Unless otherwise indicated, all herbs in recipes are fresh; we season with sea salt and freshly ground black pepper; vegetables and fruits are washed and trimmed; and vegetables such as onions, garlic, carrots, squash and potatoes are peeled.
- We always bake with golden caster sugar and unsalted butter, unless otherwise indicated in the recipe, and test all recipes with semi-skimmed milk.

Cooking tips

- Recipes are tested in conventional ovens, using oven thermometers. For fan-assisted ovens, we advise reducing the oven temperature by 10–20C.
- To skin tomatoes, use a knife to place a small cross at the base. Place in a bowl, cover with boiling water and soak for 60 seconds. Drain off the hot water, cover the tomatoes with cold water, then peel off the skins. This also works for peaches and shallots.
- To sterilise a jar, wash the jar and lid (removing rubber seal); place in the oven at 100C/gas ¼ for 30 minutes, until dry. Immerse the seal in a pan of boiling water and simmer for 10 minutes then remove with tongs. If you're reusing jam jars, wash the jars and lids, then heat in the low oven.
- We use mixing bowls made from nonreactive materials such as glass, ceramic or plastic to prevent acidic reactions from marinades.

Nutritional breakdown

The values given at the end of each recipe are based on theoretical data and cooked weight, and calculated based on tests carried out in the Jamie Oliver test kitchens. Nutritional values may vary from those published. When a recipe serves, say, 6–8, the nutritional analysis is based on the larger serving size. Serving sizes are based on the recipe's recommendations and don't generally include extras, for example, "Cream, to serve".